PAUL
THE
TEACHER

A Resource
for Teachers
in the Church

Kent L. Johnson

AUGSBURG Publishing House • Minneapolis

PAUL THE TEACHER
A Resource for Teachers in the Church

Copyright © 1986 Augsburg Publishing House

Scripture quotations unless otherwise noted are from the Revised Standard Version of the Bible, copyright 1946, 1952, and 1971 by the Division of Christian Education of the National Council of Churches.

Library of Congress Cataloging-in-Publication Data

Johnson, Kent L., 1934–
    PAUL THE TEACHER.

    1. Paul, the Apostle, Saint—Contributions in
teaching.   2. Education—History.   I. Title.
BS2506.J64   1986   207   86-17384
ISBN 0-8066-2226-1

Manufactured in the U.S.A.   APH 10-4905

1   2   3   4   5   6   7   8   9   0   1   2   3   4   5   6   7   8   9

CONTENTS

INTRODUCTION

The Paul we meet in Acts and his letters was a man of varied dimensions. He was an evangelist, theologian, apologist, and organizer of the church. In addition, and at the same time he was all the others, he was a teacher. That is in no way surprising. The world in which he lived was one already rich in educational traditions. His own background was no exception. As early as the fourth century B.C., the Jews had conceived of the synagogue, and its school, as a means of incorporating their young into the traditions of Israel. By A.D. 70 formal education had been made mandatory for all young Jewish males.

Centuries before Paul was born, Plato's *Republic* had already become an educational classic. The perfect society proposed by the famed philosopher was dependent, as described in the book, on an educational system that equipped all members of the society to function at the highest level of their ability—for the sake of the whole. After Plato there was no shortage of educational theorists in the Greco-Roman world who added their opinions about the proper practice and purpose of education. Closer to Paul's own day, Plutarch and Quintilian wrote extensively on the subject and were generally recognized as experts on the subject of teaching and learning.

Without intending to belittle their significant insights and contributions, it is a fact that outside of classes in the history and philosophy of education, the names of Plutarch and Quintilian are hardly known today. At the same time, the name of their contemporary, Paul, is one of the most oft-repeated among those gathered to study the Christian faith. Because of the authority of his letters, his words and thoughts find their way into the services of Christians who come together to worship in places all over the earth. Through what he wrote, Paul became, and remains, a respected teacher for millions today.

Initially, however, Paul gained his identity as a teacher not only because he wrote letters, but because he taught. He was himself, in his actions and purpose, a teacher. As already noted, this is not at all amazing. The one to whom he had given his life had been a teacher. As a product of a much-refined practice of education, and living in a time that honored learning as few other eras have, what vocation would have been more likely to claim his talents? And, given the purpose of his life's work—that of making known the revelation of God in Jesus Christ and applying that revelation to the whole of life—what other vocation could Paul have chosen? Based on his letters and Acts, the first purpose of this study is to give some definition to Paul's ministry as a teacher. That task, however, is not without its problems.

Paul certainly knew he was a teacher, but not in a self-conscious sort of way. No one had particularly designated him as such. He wasn't preoccupied with what teachers do, or how they are supposed to behave. Paul wasn't what one could call a "professional." He simply wanted to make known the revelation that had come to him. To do that he *had* to teach. Unfortunately, there exist no known documents that describe either Paul's physical appearance or specific ways that he went about his teaching. It just isn't possible, therefore, to describe Paul in this study as an observer of his teaching might have. It is possible, however, to examine his letters and Acts in the light of several issues that men like Plutarch and Quintilian dealt with in their day—questions that teachers continue to explore today. They are the questions that relate to style, to purpose, to the nature of the learner, and to learning itself. Responses to these questions may not actually describe how teachers will interact with those they teach, but they do provide the framework out of which teachers do their work. Perhaps that is the best we can hope for in getting some impression of Paul's ministry as a teacher.

A second purpose of this study is to provide a resource for present teachers in the church as they examine these same questions and compare their responses to those I have attributed to Paul. In doing so, readers are encouraged to question and challenge the portrait of Paul given in the following pages. Even more, they are invited to make their own judgments about Paul's responses to the issues that are raised and to wonder if they are the most appropriate ones for teachers in the church today. Readers should make no apology if they find themselves disagreeing with Paul at some points. After all, teaching is not an exact science. In addition, Paul took it upon himself to critique and evaluate others. For example, he didn't like what he saw in John Mark while they were together on the first missionary journey. Later, when Barnabas wanted to take Mark along on another journey, Paul refused to allow it. He was so adamant about the matter, as was Barnabas, that the two men parted company for a time (Acts 15:36ff.). John Mark wasn't the only one to come under the scrutiny of Paul. Others, however, like Timothy, fared much better (1 Thess. 3:1ff.). It should also be noted that Paul could change his mind, as he did in the case of John Mark. In any case, I think Paul would have welcomed a critique of himself, especially if it led to our growth as teachers. To assist in that process, questions for reflection and discussion have been included at the close of each chapter.

IDENTIFYING
THE
TEACHER

Around the base of the dome of St. Paul's Cathedral in London are statues of many of the church's great teachers. Above the statues, painted on the walls of the dome itself, are scenes from the life of the apostle for whom the cathedral is named. In this magnificent setting artists have portrayed Paul as a teacher of the great teachers of the church.

The planners of the cathedral were consistent with Acts, Paul's epistles, and the history of the church. Throughout his life in Christ, and in the pages of his letters, Paul taught and continues to teach. Second only to Jesus and the Gospels, the church has turned to him for instruction. But what kind of a teacher was he? Some, with a more critical bent, might want to rephrase that question to ask: Was Paul really a teacher? The beginnings of an answer to both questions are found in how one defines teaching. From among the many definitions that could be noted, only two are outlined here: the enabling and authority approaches. Two others, the authoritarian and the laissez-faire approaches, are introduced briefly as aberrations of the authority and enabling models.

Teachers as Enablers

In recent years several synonyms have been introduced that describe one view of what a teacher is and does: guide, facilitator, and enabler. In this view learners and their needs are the necessary centers of the educational process. Each learner must have the freedom and opportunity to develop his or her uniqueness. The teacher's responsibility is to assist students in their development. This style of teaching is characterized by an openness to student suggestions and a sense of equality between all parties linked together for the purpose of learning. Methods used in this approach emphasize inquiry, discovery, exploration, problem solving, and openness. While this model seems to stress the value of the individual almost to the exclusion of groups or institutions, that is not necessarily the case. Teachers using this model may have socialization as their primary aim.

Some have interpreted the enabling model as one that requires the teacher to surrender all authority in the educational enterprise. From this perspective, teachers hardly dare give any directions to a class for fear of infringing upon the rights and needs of learners. Giving information, especially in the form of a lecture, is especially inappropriate. As a sign of the equality between teachers and learners, teachers do not occupy positions at the head of the class. Most generally they remain seated among their students and, according to at least one parody of the position, continuously ask two questions: What do *you* think? (without ever giving their own opinions) and What would *you* like to do today? The you in both cases, of course, is the learner. The critics of this approach, which they have named laissez-faire, tend to ask the question: Who is in charge in such an educational setting? The answer seems to be no one.

While there certainly are aspects of the enabler in the teaching of Paul, I've never heard of him being accused as being laissez-faire. That simply was not his way of going about teaching. Quite the contrary, his overall approach leaned in another direction, that of the teacher as authority.

Teachers as Authorities

Another view of teaching, around for a longer period of time and thus labeled traditional, is quite different from that of the enabler. According to this view all students are perceived as having needs that can be identified by teachers and/or others in authority. The purpose of education in meeting those needs is to assist students in gaining an identity consistent with the institution that sponsors it. Essentially the teacher is a servant of the institution, and if not of the institution as such, a servant of an idea or principle to which the teacher adheres.

In both the enabler and authority models there is the possibility of confusing means with ends. For the enabler, who values process, there is the inclination to make process an end in itself. Teachers in the authority model tend to value content. Their tendency is to identify teaching/learning of content—whether it be information, skills, or attitudes—as the end of education. Whether or not it becomes that end, content does assume a larger place in the style of teachers who emphasize the authority model over against those who see themselves as enablers. Of the two, it is the authority model that more closely describes Paul's approach to his teaching ministry. That is not to say, however, that he was without characteristics associated with enablers. The evidence indicates that Paul made use of both approaches. Interestingly, current research suggests that those teachers who do use both are generally more effective than those who depend on one or the other.[1]

---

[1]David L. Silvernail, *Teaching Styles as Related to Student Achievement.* (Washington, D.C.: National Education Association, 1979), pp. 12-15.

Paul: A Representative of the Authority-Enabler Model

The apostle Paul could not be placed among those who would argue for a single model of teaching. As it will be more fully illustrated in later chapters, there were many characteristics of the enabler in his teaching. Let it be sufficient here to point out that Paul was concerned for process *and* the learner. He recognized that it wasn't helpful to approach every person and situation in the same way, and therefore he accommodated himself to fit the contexts in which he taught. He invited discussion on what he had taught and allowed for opposing opinions. His whole understanding of himself as a servant who could preach and teach the gospel, but who could not force faith into the hearts and lives of others, points to Paul as an enabler. While this dimension of his teaching cannot be ignored, it is also clear that Paul could not rest comfortably among those who refer to themselves as only enablers—for several reasons.

First, he was not very adept at setting out alternatives from which his hearers were free to choose. He was more apt to say, as he wrote to the Corinthians:

> According to the grace of God given to me, like a skilled master builder I laid a foundation. . . . Let each man take care how he builds upon it. For no other foundation can any one lay than that which is laid, which is Christ Jesus (1 Cor. 3:10-11).

Neither is it likely that Paul could have separated himself or his purpose from the content he taught. So closely did he identify himself with his message that he wrote: "I have been crucified with Christ; it is no longer I who live, but Christ who lives in me; and the life I now live in the flesh I live by faith in the Son of God, who loved me and gave himself for me" (Gal. 2:20). Paul wanted his learners to make that same identification (Rom. 6:1-4). That there was no doubt in his mind as to the specificity of this content, and its appropriateness for all in the church, is evident in Paul's strong words to the Galatians:

> I am astonished that you are so quickly deserting him who called you in the grace of Christ and turning to a different gospel—not that there is another gospel, but there are some who trouble you and want to pervert the gospel of Christ. But even if we, or an angel from heaven, should preach to you a gospel contrary to that which we preached to you, let him be accursed. As we have said before, so now I say again, if any one is preaching to you a gospel contrary to that which you received, let him be accursed (Gal. 1:6-9).

Finally, though Paul most often introduced himself as a servant, he didn't hesitate to claim that he was also an authority. In response to those who challenged his apostleship, he claimed that his came directly from God (Gal. 1:1). He was not afraid to claim equal status with anyone—even the pillars of the church (Gal. 2:9). Those in Corinth who questioned his insights and decisions were reminded that it was Paul who had founded the church among them and therefore had a rightful claim as an authority (2 Cor. 10:1ff.). And, though there were times when he admitted that what he was writing was really his opinion (1 Cor. 6:12ff.), most often he spoke and wrote with confidence and authority concerning the message he was presenting to others (1 Cor. 7:39-40; 15:1ff.).

Paul would have described teachers as ones who shared with others what they believed to be true and who did so in a way that assisted others to learn and come to the same conviction. With respect to the former, Paul's approach was that of an authority. With respect to the notion that he assisted others to learn, he was an enabler. Recognizing, however, that Paul's end was predetermined, and that by him, weights his overall approach on the side of the authority model. There are considerable risks involved when teachers do weight their teaching on the side of the authority model. The greatest risk is that it can lead to teachers taking too much control of the learning of others. It is the mistake of assuming that the teacher always knows what is best for the student and using a position of power to force submission. It is the misguided notion that the uniqueness of persons must be sacrificed for the sake of what all have in common. It is the denial of creativity, inquiry, and discovery. When this risk has become a reality, the authoritarian model of education exists.

The authoritarian model, in deceptive and cruel hands, has been the means of denying the worth and individuality of countless persons. More than is likely ever to be known, it has contributed to the enslavement of nations and conflicts between nations. It is an understanding of education and teaching that is associated with words and actions many educators abhor: closed, indoctrination, and sectarian. In order to avoid the excesses associated with this aberration of the authority model, it's understandable there are those who would prefer to eliminate the authority model altogether as an alternative for teaching. At least in part the popularity of the enabler model is the result of such a desire.

Paul and the Authoritarian Approach

While there may be none to accuse Paul of being laissez-faire, there are those who would bring against him the charge of authoritarianism. Though it is true that the church and some of its teachers have used that approach, there is no need to conclude that Paul did the same or would have encouraged those who did. The evidence in the New Testament points to just the opposite conclusion. One could, of course, speculate as to how Paul might have functioned during the time of the church's political ascendancy. It's more helpful, though, to examine what he did and wrote and to understand both in the context in which he lived. When that is done, Paul is seen as one who defined teaching in authority/enabler rather than authoritarian terms.

First, there is Paul's conviction that he could not achieve, or in any way force, the end for which he worked. If any teacher was ever aware of his limitations, and the limitations on his students' abilities to learn, it was Paul. He was convinced that he could not create faith, bring about spiritual understanding, or incorporate others into the family of God. All of this came about through the power of the Holy Spirit (1 Cor. 2:6ff.; 12:3). Much of Paul's teaching was done among nonbelievers. In such a situation a demand for conformity and total acceptance of what he taught would have contradicted an essential aspect of his theology.

Second, the world in which Paul lived was essentially pluralistic. It was a world in which many ideas and beliefs vied for allegiance, with none, save obedience to Rome, dominant. Such a context places limitations upon an authoritarian view of teaching. Acts and the Epistles provide ample evidence that Paul was aware of his situation—the most obvious being the importance he attached to teaching and nurture. He was not satisfied with a superficial understanding of the gospel or an easy acquiescence to it on the part of those he taught. He worked hard to root believers firmly in the gospel in order that they could grow. In some communities he settled down for more than a year, spending much of his time teaching. He wrote letters of encouragement and correction to those congregations from which he was separated. He kept them constantly in his prayers. In later years, when the church was the dominant force in Western Europe, its teachers didn't exhibit that same concern for nurture. The church had its way without nurturing its people, simply because it was in a position of power. Paul's situation was just the opposite. He recognized that if the church was to remain alive in a pluralistic society, it had to grow, and he knew it could grow through teaching.

Paul was also aware that in his world he could not control the thinking of those he taught. He could not even guarantee the faithfulness of those who had been converted to the gospel. In his closing words to the Ephesian elders, Paul informed them that they would have to assume responsibility for the gospel they had been taught. Paul had done all that he could (Acts 20:25ff.). There is ambiguity in such situations. While there is anxiety for the beloved, there is also the recognition that one must, in a pluralistic environment, be able to stand in the midst of different and conflicting opinions. People who have been controlled by an external force are not well prepared to face that kind of challenge.

Closely related to the above was Paul's awareness that he wasn't the only one concerned for the faith and life of others. The world seemed to be filled with teachers expounding ideas that clamored for attention. Some of these teachers would scoff at the gospel and encourage others to do the same. Paul knew of Judaizers who entangled the gospel in the law and who pointed to Paul as a heretic. There were those, too, who welcomed the gospel only because it seemed to serve their personal ends; Paul knew of these as well. These views, and many more, were viable ways of looking at the gospel Paul preached, just as they are possibilities in the pluralistic societies of today. Their adherents, in Paul's day no more than in our own, couldn't be burned at the stake or in some other way removed from the scene. They were simply there, and Paul knew they had to be more than endured. His intent was to defend the church against them, and the best defense was a sound theology based on the gospel and taught by those who were its servants.

Paul's Identification with the Authority-Enabler Model

There is considerable evidence that Paul didn't come to the authority-enabler model "naturally." Whatever its source in the human species, Paul in his youth and early adulthood had a sharp competitive edge to his personality. He had a strong desire to excel, and excel he did. His energies were channeled into his studies. As he wrote to both the Corinthians and Galatians, he was a better student than most of his peers, and as a result he became a Hebrew among Hebrews—one who was at the head of his class (2 Cor. 11:22; Gal. 1:14). Though there wasn't anything wrong with this, the desire to excel was translated, in his early adult years, into a desire to dominate—to compel others, if necessary, to conform to the Mosaic traditions as he understood them. Having access to the kind of authority that could put teeth into his desires, he set about to coerce that conformity, specifically to destroy the circle of people who confessed Jesus of Nazareth as the Messiah.

The picture of Saul standing on the periphery of the crowd, consenting as Stephen was stoned to death, is a somber reminder of the power of ideas and of those who wield that power against others (Acts 7:54ff.). Saul had not been a military figure; he was a scholar. He had not been shaped on the battlefield, but in the classroom. It was as a scholar, molded by his studies, that Saul went about his work persecuting the early church. So convinced was he of the rightness of his position that he could consent to the death of those who disagreed with him. An extreme case, but an example nevertheless, of authoritarianism created by education. It was this identity that Paul had to live down, in the Christian community, for the rest of his life. The people he had tried to persecute simply had a hard time believing that he could change, but change he did.

The story of Saul's conversion on the road to Damascus is a familiar one (Acts 9:1ff.). The effects of the experience on his life and thought are evident in his influence upon the Christian community in the first century and in his letters that express his confident faith in Jesus as the promised Messiah. Not least, Paul changed in his understanding of his life's work and how he was to go about it. He abandoned the use of force and intimidation as means of gaining his own ends. He adopted a vocation for which his earlier excellence as a student had admirably equipped him—he became a teacher.

Paul himself didn't dwell on how these changes in his life and thought came about. There's no reasoned discourse in his letters about how he came to realize that the authoritarian approach to teaching and persuasion of others was inappropriate for what he was called to do. After alluding to his conversion, Paul simply told the Galatians that he went away to Arabia. Presumably he went away to think through the implications of what he had seen and heard that day on the Damascus road and to consider what it meant for the faith of Israel that God's Son had been crucified on a tree and had risen (Gal. 1:17ff.).

Paul emerged from his reflections a different person. Oh, not different in every respect. He retained that drive and tenacity that had characterized his earlier life. There remained some of that competitive edge that had been so much a part of him. And, whether he was driven to excel, or was equipped by his earlier achievements to do so in a way that he could not hide, Paul did excel. What had changed most significantly was his orientation. He no longer saw himself leading the charge against heresy, willing to destroy the ones he perceived to be the enemies of God. The one Paul had met on the Damascus road was, himself, the persecuted and crucified one. From the agony of a cross Jesus had called his disciples to *follow* him. By his mercy and constant forgiveness Jesus had enabled them, however imperfectly, to do just that. Paul became the servant of this Jesus. Being a servant of the crucified and risen Lord Jesus, rather than any examined decision about how one should teach, determined Paul's approach to teaching as an authority-enabler.

His authority was grounded in his commission as a servant. He believed that he had been set aside, by God, to preach the kingdom and teach the good news of Jesus Christ (Rom. 1:1; Gal. 1:15). His authority was derived from the Lord of heaven and earth. When voices were raised to challenge him or to scoff at what he taught, he responded: ". . . I am not ashamed of the gospel: it is the power of God for salvation to everyone who has faith, to the Jew first and also to the Greek" (Rom. 1:16). And he was an enabler. That's all he could be, but that was enough. If he couldn't create faith in the hearts of his hearers, he could be the instrument of the Holy Spirit who did. In his letter to the Colossians Paul connected these two sides of his approach, the authority and enabling dimensions, that defined him as a teacher:

> Him [Jesus] we proclaim, warning every man and teaching every man in all wisdom, that we may present every man mature in Christ. For this I toil, striving with all the energy which he mightily inspires within me (Col. 1:28-29).

For Reflection

1. How do you define teaching?
2. How does your definition of teaching compare/contrast with that of Paul's described in this chapter?
3. Few, if any, teachers subscribe totally to either the authority or enabler model in their teaching. Most, however, probably lean toward one or the other. Which emphasis, do you think, is most prevalent in the church today? In your opinion, is that a healthy situation for the church? Give reasons and examples for your responses.
4. Are you aware of any laissez-faire or authoritarian-like teachers in the church? What do you see as the reasons for their adopting that model, and what are the effects upon learners?
5. Is Paul's approach to teaching the one that should/could be adopted by teachers in the church today? Why or why not?

IDENTIFYING
THE
LEARNER

"What is man that thou art mindful of him?" the psalmist asked of God more than 2000 years ago (Ps. 8:4). The question continues to be raised today—if not always asked of God, at least with enthusiasm and a desire to know the answer. There are many ways to come at the issue. Some begin from the perspective of the natural order and compare and contrast humans with other living organisms. Others describe humans in anatomical terms. Still others approach the question in psychological, philosophical, or theological terms. Whichever approach is taken, sooner or later one comes to the questions of needs, capabilities, and limitations. These are important matters, especially for teachers. How teachers respond to them influences their expectations of themselves and their students, their goals, and the way they go about teaching.

The Learner Viewed Theologically

Paul was a theologian. Everything about him—his past, education, self-understanding, work, hope, friends, and purpose—was inseparable from his beliefs about God. It would have been impossible for him to think of humankind in terms other than the theological. Therefore his response to the question What is man? must begin with his understanding of the relationship between God and humankind, and humankind and God. Neither side of the relationship can be ignored without distorting the picture.

Humankind's relationship with God was marked, Paul insisted, by an insurmountable limitation. As a result of the former's self-will and disobedience, a barrier had developed between them. The very essence of the barrier existed within humankind. It expressed itself in the desire to be what it could not be—God. This desire led to rebellion and alienation. So thorough was the alienation that humankind could do nothing to please God. So complete was the rebellion that humankind could not see God, or find its way across the chasm that separated it from God. Whatever goodness and wisdom humans could claim served only to fortify the barrier with the building blocks of pride and self-righteousness (Romans 1–3).

At the very core of the problem in the relationship with God was humankind's misguided response to the question What is man? Failing to acknowledge the creator God, humankind claimed to be God and came to worship the work of its own hands. Limited by pride and ignorance, men and women could not be at peace with God, themselves, or each other. Alienated from God, they were not alive to his righteousness. Separated from God, they were victims of the last and most terrible of enemies, death. Reconciliation, argued Paul, was humankind's greatest need, but it was a need that could not be satisfied through human effort. Who, Paul asked in his letter to the Romans, could deliver him and all humankind? (Rom. 7:24).

From his Judaic background Paul inherited the conviction that nothing was impossible for God. From the same source came the faith that God's will was being worked out in history. Only after his conversion did Paul understand that God's will was the reconciliation of all, both Jew and Gentile. Only after God's grace had transformed him did he realize that God's purpose was being achieved through love—the sacrificial love of his own Son. Given this new understanding, Paul read the Scriptures in a new light. He recognized that reconciliation had been God's intent long before Abraham. God's choosing of Abraham and raising up the nation of Israel was a sign of God's love and intention to both reveal his will and prepare for its further revelation (Romans 4).

Finally, because of his immeasurable love, God gave his Son (Rom. 5:6ff.). In his perfect obedience, especially in the cross, the love of Christ overcame all the barriers. What could be done in no other way, God accomplished. The revelation Paul had received, the secret hid for long ages, was summed up in the words: ". . . In Christ God was reconciling the world to himself . . ." (2 Cor. 5:19). Unable to achieve this reconciliation through its own efforts, humankind had only to receive it in faith, trusting in the love of God, and therein finding peace (Rom. 5:1).

The contrast between God and humans, and the nature of their relationship based on that contrast, was foremost in Paul's response to the question What is man? God is active, faithful, loving, and unlimited in power. Humankind is rebellious, jealous, and limited. Paul's adoption of an authority model for teaching was consistent with this outlook. Those he taught were like him—in need of reconciliation with God. Like him, without revelation they could not know God's love and forgiveness. Unforgiven and unloved, they could not be at peace. Limited by their very nature, there was nothing they could do to change their situation. By the authority of his calling as a servant of Christ, Paul's responsibility was to make the revelation of reconciliation known and allow it to create faith in those who heard it.

Paul Contrasted with an Authoritarian View of the Learner

Over the years many educational programs have been built on the principle of human limitations. In such approaches all knowledge tends to take the character of revelation, as though there was nothing that students could discover for themselves. In such an approach teachers are the primary actors. Students are expected to be passive. Their responsibility is to receive what their teachers give. Having received it, they are to repeat it without deviation. When they are unable to do so, they are sometimes labeled as failures. When their behavior is not passive, it is often judged as rebellious. Based on such a premise many children are punished for behavior that may be quite normal for their age, and they are sometimes criticized for not understanding concepts that are beyond their ability to comprehend. This description may be more accurate of a 19th-century understanding of the student than of any present view, but aspects of it still remain, in practice if not in theory. Unfortunately, both critics and advocates of this viewpoint look to Paul as one of the primary sources for an authoritarian model of teaching is derived from the view of the learner described above.

While it's true that his basic assumptions about human nature support such a view, Paul saw more in humankind than its limitations. For that reason, and for many more, Paul cannot be associated with an authoritarian teaching model that assumes the passivity of the learner. There is, first, the witness of his own work. Paul could not have been authoritarian even if he had wanted to be. He did not teach children in the context of compulsory education. His audience was made up of adults who could choose whether or not they would listen to him. If they disagreed with him, or he became abusive, they could always walk away. Though Paul did at least his share of talking, Acts describes a good bit of that talk as arguing. Argument assumes an exchange of ideas—activity on both sides of the conversation. And Paul describes himself as striving with tears to persuade rather than bludgeon his listeners with the gospel (2 Cor. 2:4). Little in Paul's approach suggests a teacher who had, and exercised, control over passive learners.

Second, the authoritarian approach, at least as practiced by some in the church, has emphasized too much human limitations and too little God's power. If Romans 1, 3, and 4 are faithful representations of Paul's thought, so are Romans 5 and 8. In the latter chapter Paul wrote of God's love for his creation that was so great he sent his Son to die for his beloved. The power of this act of love overcame death and all the forces of evil. There was nothing in all creation that could stand against it. If God loved humankind in this way, could he, Paul, have despised it? If Jesus was willing to suffer and die for sinful humanity, could Paul have rationalized an approach that reversed the process—the suffering of students for the sake of teachers? Could Paul, who had tried so hard to model his life after Jesus, desert that model at the crucial point of his teaching? I think not.

Of course, there must have been times when Paul's human limitations became only too obvious. He must be believed when he wrote that he was not able to do the very things he wanted to do (Rom. 7:13ff.). With all his limitations, however, it's hardly possible that he would have functioned as a teacher in a manner that contradicted his belief in God's love for a fallen creation. Indeed, it was this love that constrained him to do what he did (2 Cor. 5:14). Paul's capacity for reason was too great to allow for such a contradiction.

The authoritarian model also contradicts the notion of humankind being the crown of God's creation. If limited with respect to a relationship with God, humans could still think and be creative in many ways. Paul doesn't deny this. In fact, he sees it as part of the problem, but it's something that he doesn't dismiss simply because it can be distorted. On the other hand, once the Spirit had entered a person's life these qualities became tremendous resources for pleasing God. In describing these qualities one gets a more complete picture of Paul's view of the learner.

Learners are active.   That Paul saw action as a human trait can be illustrated in several ways. Learners are, for example, actively curious. He saw this quality in those of Athens who were always searching for something new. On many occasions, his method of teaching assumed that he could capture the curiosity of his hearers and, having done so, tell them the gospel. When he stood before Felix, Festus, and Agrippa, he must have thought they were curious to know about him, for he didn't hesitate to tell them his story, or the gospel. Paul didn't see this curiosity as an enemy. Though it may not be the best word for it, curiosity suggests a quality that leads to a quest for God.

From another perspective, this curiosity had led to a search for understanding the natural world, the world of human affairs, and the world of mind and body—with all the imponderables associated with each. Blessed by the Spirit of God, this searching widens the door to the praise of God for the wonders of creation.

Another side to human activity in Paul's thought is creativity. In spite of alienation from God, this quality was not lost to human activity. Paul walked the streets of Athens as well as Jerusalem. He saw the architectural and artistic work done by the hands of the Greeks. I don't think he would have tried to deny that these represented a capacity for creativity. As a son of Abraham, and a citizen of Rome, he knew and appreciated the laws that allowed a society to govern itself—laws that could be either freeing or limiting, but, in either case, an expression of creativity.

Paul was also aware that creativity was a part of the human problem—especially as it was invested in the making of gods. The Athenians combined logic with their artistic ability in the building of an altar to an unknown god, just to be sure that all their obligations with respect to the gods could be met. Paul, interestingly, didn't scold these people for what they had done. Instead, he used it as a means of introducing to them something they had not previously known—the gospel of Jesus Christ.

To be sure, Paul was convinced that outside of Christ, creativity—no matter how helpful or beautiful it might be—could not please God. But in Christ it became one of the freeing aspects of the gospel. For those living "in Christ" the law no longer dictated specific behaviors. They were free, and responsible, to both initiate and respond to situations with all the creativity that was theirs. By the Spirit, the fruits of gentleness, kindness, goodness, and self-control could take on infinite variety in the moment where need and ability came together (Gal. 5:22-23).

Paul recognized, and anticipated, human activity in all areas of life—service, worship, and thought. As noted already, he was convinced his learners could think. He expected them to draw conclusions from what he had taught them and from the experiences of their lives. Without that confidence Paul's work as a teacher would have been hopeless. He knew a time would come when those he taught would have to make decisions and respond to the challenges put to the faith. Eventually there would be no Paul—nor an Apollos nor a Cephas. He exhorted the people of Corinth to live under the lordship of Jesus, and not to be dependent upon any human teacher (1 Cor. 3:5ff.). Such a challenge would make no sense if Paul didn't think his learners could respond to it.

Paul encouraged the Romans to think of their lives as an ongoing worship of God. That life, as Paul described it, could be nothing less than creatively active through the power of the Holy Spirit. He wrote:

> . . . present your bodies as a living sacrifice, holy and acceptable to God, which is your spiritual worship. Do not be conformed to this world but be transformed by the renewal of your mind, that you may prove what is the will of God, what is good and acceptable and perfect (Rom. 12:1-2).

Nearly 2000 years after Paul, persons such as Jean Piaget have come to the conclusion that activity—interaction between persons and their environments—is a primary factor in learning. In a marvelous way Paul anticipated this in his recognition of the possibilities and importance of human activity. He didn't credit all of it as being good, but seeing its potential for evil didn't lead to his denial of its importance in learning. On the contrary, knowing its potential as a problem, Paul was all the more eager to turn those possibilities in a positive direction through the transforming power of the Holy Spirit.

Learners have worth in their differences.　Paul wasn't the first to discover that there are differences among people, or what educators like to call "individual differences." He was, however, among the first to argue that these differences did not justify prejudice. In fact, Paul celebrated differences as a reflection of the creative glory of God and as means by which the mission of the church could be accomplished. This view had its basis in Paul's understanding of the work of Jesus Christ.

As a Jew, Paul found himself supporting a case that has for centuries been reversed. He found it necessary to demonstrate to Jews that in Christ God had redeemed all the world, that Gentiles were, with them, the beloved of God. Jews, he said, had to accept Gentiles on the basis of God's love, not on the condition that they first observe the laws and traditions of the Jews.

Once Paul understood that there was nothing inherently superior about either Jews or Gentiles, he began to apply that principle to other categories. In Christ, he wrote, there is neither male or female, slave or free—all have equal status before God without the necessity of one becoming like the other (Gal. 3:28). It may have been a small beginning as some would view it, but it started a process that can lead to accepting learners where they are and helping them to learn what they are able to learn. Paul accepted all people, and he had good reason. In Christ there are no distinctions.

Paul's acceptance of differences is evident in the relationships he had with all kinds of people. His message and boldness were the same whether he was talking to a Lydia, a Roman governor, a Philippian jailer, soldiers, Jews in a marketplace or in their synagogue, or the chosen disciples of Jesus. His approach obviously varied, but that only further illustrates his acceptance of differences. As he wrote to the Corinthians, he was willing to become all things to all people in order that he might win some to the gospel.

It is the nature of authoritarians to make others fit their image. Paul's objective was not that; his intent was to have all conform to the image of Christ. This image, in Paul's thought, was capable of tremendous variety. To sanctify each in his or her own identity to the image of Christ, rather than recasting all humanity into a single mold, was Paul's understanding of the Spirit's work. He did not go far in theorizing about the implications of his thought for education, but he grasped the principle and founded it securely on the gospel. Others would have to work out those implications. It's a wonder that it should have taken so long.

Learners are capable of change.   There is considerable confusion about how, and to what extent, humans change. This confusion has a long history. Centuries before researchers charted the stages of physical, moral, and psychological development, parents were aware that their children went through phases. They may not have understood why, or how best to respond to them, but they observed them all the same. In spite of that awareness, social conventions evolved that denied the possibilities for certain kinds of change. Thomas Hardy's novel *Jude the Obscure* tells of the frustration experienced by a young man who tried to defy the rules of social class. Strict conventions about where a person belongs as a factor of birth—whether they are rules of 19th-century Christian Europe, or present-day Hindu India—are based on the notion that humans don't change. At least some of the Spanish conquistadores justified the extermination of native peoples on the basis that they were different and could not change. The institution of slavery, especially as practiced in America, probably had the same foundation. In the minds of at least some, black people were born to be slaves, and that didn't change.

While the above examples represent extreme views on the subject of the ability, or inability, of humans to change, there are less violent ones that are still given some credence today. For example, some adults resort to the expression "you can't teach an old dog new tricks" as a justification for their unwillingness to try something new. "A leopard can't change its spots" is the reason given by some for not being open to the possibility that delinquents can change their outlook and behavior. After seeing little of its evidence in their students, some teachers have been known to give up on their expectations for change, thus short-circuiting the educational process. All of these examples are simply to point out that there isn't universal agreement, even today, with regard to the learner's ability to change.

Paul was convinced of the reality of change. After all, his own life had been completely turned around after his Damascus road experience. How could he deny change in the lives of others? (It's interesting that Paul was a victim of the thinking that denied change. Not a few in the early church had a great deal of difficulty in accepting Paul as an apostle. They couldn't forget the Saul who had raised so much havoc among them. Could they really trust him? Was his conversion for real? were questions that followed him throughout his life. Charles Colson's acceptance by the church, apparently, is a contemporary example of the same thing.) Rather than denying change, Paul expected it. As noted earlier, he repeatedly exhorted his people to grow—growth being another word for positive change. He wrote to the Corinthians: "And we all, with unveiled face, beholding the glory of the Lord, are being changed into his likeness from one degree of glory to another. . ." (2 Cor. 3:18). This change, said Paul, came from ". . . the Lord who is the Spirit."

Paul didn't seem interested in guessing who the persons would be in whom God would bring about change. Believing he had to wait and trust God to work the miracle of faith, he adopted the only posture really open to him. He became a preacher and teacher, confidently expecting that wherever God chose, the miracle would happen. He neither selected one group as more likely to be receptive or eliminated another because of an apparent determination not to change. (Although it is true that his rejection by the Jews kept pushing him in the direction of working among the Gentiles.) Paul went about his work with anticipation in spite of all the difficulties he encountered. His confidence was rooted in several things. First and foremost was his conviction that in Christ God had changed the world. Since the coming of Jesus, the world would never be the same. Second, the newness brought by this change was being extended into the lives of people through the power of the Holy Spirit. By God's Spirit humans could now call God "Father." Third, the grace of God was transforming the lives of those who had been dead in their sins into the new life in Christ. Paul himself had experienced it. Finally, but not least, he looked forward to the moment when everything would be changed—in the twinkling of an eye. Pointing to that day, Paul wrote:

> For the trumpet will sound, and the dead will be raised imperishable, and we shall be changed. For this perishable nature must put on the imperishable, and this mortal nature must put on immortality (1 Cor. 15:52-53).

Change, for Paul, was integral to creation and human existence. It would be difficult to imagine that it would not have figured into his view of the learner and his approach to education. It's not at all likely that he could have supported an exclusively conserving role for education. At its worst, the status quo was alien to God. At its best it failed to anticipate in hope and trust the activity of God in history and in the lives of individual persons. Without change there could be no movement toward the coming kingdom.

In Christ God had changed the world. Through the Holy Spirit God was changing the world. For teachers to deny or ignore this, or the capacity of humans to change, would be, in the thinking of Paul, to align themselves with those who frustrate the intent of God.

There are many dimensions to Paul's response to the question What is man? His response begins with the assumption of human sin and limitation. This has to be recognized as basic to Paul's understanding of human nature and the premise for the model of teaching that he adopted. This dimension alone, however, can lead to an authoritarian teaching model and/or a highly pessimistic attitude toward the human capacity for change. Paul was not pessimistic. He had unbounded confidence in God's love and wisdom. When he looked at those he taught, he saw persons God loved and for whom God had given his Son. In them he saw the *Imago Dei.* They were capable of a wide variety of activity— including service, worship, and thought. As he looked at them he saw variety, and in that variety the wisdom and creativity of God was revealed. Whatever they were, God had made possible their adoption as his children. This understanding of the learner must have made teaching a wondrous, exciting, and challenging vocation for Paul.

For Reflection

1. What are some words or phrases that describe you as a learner? If you are a teacher, how would you describe those you teach?
2. How might the teacher's perception of the learner influence the way she or he goes about teaching:
   a. in terms of expectations?
   b. in terms of activities?
   c. in terms of classroom climate and relationships?
3. Martin Luther described our human condition as one in which we are, at the same time, saints and sinners. How might that understanding influence the relationship between teachers and their students?
4. How do your responses to questions 1-3 compare/contrast with Paul's perceptions of the learner presented in this study?

CHAPTER THREE ═══════════════════

PURPOSE
IN PAUL'S
TEACHING

A few years ago my mother told me that she had found some things in her attic that belonged to me, and she wanted me to have them. Not telling me what they were, she handed me a box that I promptly took home and, without looking into it, put away in one of my closets. There it remained for at least a year. Then one day, as I was going through some things, I came across the box and decided to take a look into it. On the top was an old Boy Scout neckerchief that I had worn 35 years before. I remembered buying and wearing it. I also found a Scout belt that I can't imagine I ever wore—yet there it was, with my name accusingly printed on it.

Next I came across some cards bound together with a rubber band. The first recorded my enrollment on the cradle roll of Zion Lutheran Church, Rockford, Illinois. There were other cards, too, noting the congregation's awareness of my growing years. Finally, on the bottom of the box was a slightly crumpled certificate of attendance awarded to me in September 1941. I don't remember receiving it, but I would guess that I must have been quite proud of it at the time. I'm even more proud of it now. In fact, I had it framed and it now hangs on a wall in my study. Don't get me wrong. I'm not proud today as I might have been when I was seven, or because of what the certificate says about me. Actually it says nothing about me, aside from the fact that as a child I was rather healthy. It says a great deal, however, about my parents who saw to it that I and my six brothers and sisters were regularly present in the church school. I don't know if they ever thought much about it, but they must have had some purpose in mind that sustained them in their efforts over the some 35 years between the time my oldest brother began Sunday school and my youngest sister was confirmed.

The certificate is also a commentary on those who signed it: E. G. Knock, the pastor; Gust Swanson, the superintendent; and Lucille Lindall, the secretary. During my growing years these people assumed considerable responsibility for the religious education of the people in my home congregation. I wonder how often they were thanked. I hope someone thanked them for me, because I'm pretty sure that I didn't. I wonder if it would have occurred to me, at the age of seven, to be appreciative for teachers and Sunday school. Yet, over many years, those people gave of their time and talents. Why?

It's a good thing to be grateful for teachers, and for educational ministry in the church, but there must be some other reason than gratitude that motivates teachers. I wish I could ask Pastor Knock or Gust Swanson or Lucille Lindall why they continued in their ministry over so many years, but I can't. Unable to ask them, I've asked others who teach today: Why do you do it? Not long ago I met with a group of teachers from Marshall, Minnesota, and asked them that question. Their responses varied. One said she taught because it was a way to influence the future. Another saw it as a responsibility. Others spoke of their love for children and God's love for them. Whatever their response, all had given the question some thought.

I wonder if there are any teachers who, particularly after a difficult class when things have not gone well, haven't asked themselves the question Why do I do this? Well, whatever prompts it, that just might be the most important question that teachers can ask of themselves and of the church: What is the purpose for teaching? A solid, thoughtful response gives teachers a direction in which to go and keeps them going in their ministry whether teaching is discouraging, encouraging, or both.

Paul was a teacher with purpose. That purpose guided his activities and words as he lived out his ministry in Christ. It supported him when he was severely tested by both his foes and friends, and it kept him focused on those occasions when he could have become euphoric over his accomplishments. Before considering that purpose in Paul's teaching, a few comments need to be made concerning his understanding of God's purpose in Christ.

Paul's Understanding of God's Purpose in Christ

In the previous chapter I noted that Paul was frequently challenged with respect to his apostleship—that there were many who had a hard time accepting his conversion as real. Though that must have been a problem for him in his ministry, having to defend himself in his letters provides us with significant insights into his self-understanding and purpose. For example, Paul's authority in Galatia was a primary issue involved in the resolution of two significantly different theological perspectives. In defending his apostleship, Paul also gave expression to the purpose of his work. He wrote:

But . . . he who had set me apart before I was born, and had called me through his grace, was pleased to reveal his Son to me, in order that I might preach him among the Gentiles. . . (Gal. 1:15ff.)

Who was this Son God had revealed? What had he been all about? The first question Paul never seems to have tired of reflecting, speaking, and writing about. One of the more beautiful expressions of his understanding of Jesus is found in Colossians, where he wrote:

> He [Jesus] is the image of the invisible God, the first-born of all creation; for in him all things were created, in heaven and on earth, visible and invisible, whether thrones or dominions or principalities or authorities—all things were created through him and for him. He is before all things, and in him all things hold together. He is the head of the body, the church; he is the beginning, the first-born from the dead, that in everything he might be preeminent. For in him all the fullness of God was pleased to dwell, and through him to reconcile to himself all things, whether on earth or in heaven, making peace by the blood of his cross (Col. 1:15ff.).

By the time Paul had reached the conclusion of his thoughts about the identity of Jesus, he had already begun his answer to the question What was God about in sending him? The work of Jesus, wrote Paul, was to reconcile and make peace between God and God's creation. That theme is repeated over and over again throughout Paul's letters. How that reconciling work was accomplished was given classic expression in his letter to the Corinthians:

> For I delivered to you as of first importance what I also received, that Christ died for our sins in accordance with the scriptures, that he was buried, that he was raised on the third day in accordance with the scriptures. . . (1 Cor. 15:3ff.).

It was this revelation that had changed Paul's life. It became the center of his reflections and teaching concerning God's purpose in Christ.

The Purposes of Revelation and Response

Paul had received a revelation. His response to it changed his life as he obediently followed where his faith in the resurrected Lord Jesus led him. These two—making known the revelation and calling for the response of faith—became primary purposes in Paul's teaching ministry.

Making known the mystery of God.   The first, and most obvious, purpose that guided Paul in his teaching was making known that God had revealed himself in Jesus. This was the greatest of wonders—that God could be born in human flesh, that the promised Messiah was not one who spoke for God, but God's own Son. Then, that he should come not only in human form, but as a servant; that was a twist that the Gentiles could hardly imagine. Equally unexpected among the Jews was the discovery that the Savior was one for all humankind—for both Jews and Gentiles. And that the Messiah should suffer and die seemed either a stumbling block or folly to just about everybody. Yet this was the revelation that had come to Paul. He never got over that. Being the one to receive the revelation was about as amazing to Paul as the incarnation itself. Having received it, the purpose of his life was to make it known. He wrote to the Colossians:

> . . . I became a minister according to the divine office which was given to me for you, to make the word of God fully known, the mystery hidden for ages and generations, but now made manifest to his saints. To them God chose to make known how great among the Gentiles are the riches of the glory of this mystery, which is Christ in you, the hope of glory (Col. 1:25ff.).

The good news Paul taught was that in Christ God had reconciled the world unto himself (2 Cor. 5:19). That reconciliation became a reality in the lives of persons when it was received in faith. Paul had said that not only in Corinth, but in Galatia as well. His letter to the Galatians is an expression of his concern and his deep hurt that his teaching was being twisted in such a way that it was no longer the good news he intended it to be. Paul had taught these people that justification was by faith in the mercy of God. When the Jews in that congregation had asked whether or not the keeping of the law was still necessary for them, Paul had said no—especially with respect to circumcision. Apparently his answer had been accepted. After Paul left Galatia to continue on his missionary journeys, other teachers came along who disagreed with Paul. They were persuasive enough to cause confusion in the congregation and finally to raise a challenge to Paul's authority as a teacher of the gospel. The presence of these teachers and their disagreement with Paul provided the occasion for the letter which, in turn, is an outline of what Paul had originally taught these people.

With respect to the law, Paul wrote, its purpose had never been that of justification. It had come as a result of human transgression—to be a custodian of those who were in sin. But justification had always been a gift of God to be received in faith. Paul supported his argument by pointing to Abraham. The father of Israel, wrote Paul, had been made righteous by faith. All those who live by faith in the promises of God are descendants of Abraham and, like him, heirs of God's grace. This was true, Paul continued, whether a person was Jew or Gentile, slave or free, male or female (Gal. 3:23ff.).

In the requirement of circumcision, Paul saw the not-so-subtle implication that before Gentiles could become Christians, they must first become Jews. Circumcision itself, and especially requiring it of the Gentiles, was in Paul's mind a dependence upon the law. As soon as one allowed that requirement, he argued, the gospel had been sacrificed for the hope of justification in the law. That Paul would not allow. Those who subscribed to that teaching were severed from Christ (Gal. 5:4). Those who taught such doctrines were called false teachers and Paul called down a curse upon them (Gal. 1:9).

Galatians demonstrates the radical change that came about in Paul's theology following the Damascus road experience. At one time he had been a zealous defender of the Mosaic tradition. After the revelation, he came to the realization that justification was God's gift, and that it had always been received by faith. All of Paul's letters have the same theme. In his introduction to the letter to the Romans he was especially clear about his intent. He wrote that he was ". . . under obligation both to Greeks and to barbarians, both to the wise and to the foolish . . ." to make known the gospel he had received. It was a gospel of which he could not be ashamed (Rom. 1:14ff). Then, without the rancor of Galatians, and in a more complete way, Paul laid out for the people in Rome the essential content of his teaching. It is risky to suggest that any single passage adequately summarizes Paul's understanding of the gospel, but if there is one that does it as well as any other, it would be the fifth chapter of his letter to these Romans:

> Since we are justified by faith, we have peace with God through our Lord Jesus Christ. Through him we have obtained access to this grace in which we stand, and we rejoice in our hope of sharing the glory of God (Rom. 5:1-2).

Paul's commitment to the purpose of making the gospel known is illustrated in the dramatic moment he stood, a prisoner, before King Agrippa and the Roman governor, Festus. Agrippa invited Paul to speak. The apostle used the occasion to rehearse the events of the time when the revelation had first come to him. He claimed that he had only been obedient to that revelation, and for that he had been persecuted and threatened with death—even when that revelation was consistent with the teachings of Moses and the prophets.

The king responded to Paul's presentation: "In a short time you think to make me a Christian!" Paul continued: "Whether short or long, I would to God that not only you but also all who hear me this day might become such as I am—except for these chains" (Acts 26:1ff.). Paul's teaching began and ended in his own obedience to the gospel, to the revelation that he had received. Once he had made it known to others, as in the case noted above, Paul looked for the response of faith. The response of faith is the second, or the other side of the first, purpose in Paul's teaching.

The Outcome of Faith.   Once Paul had made known the gospel to others, he anticipated some results in them. He didn't just speak the words describing the revelation and let it go at that. He had some expectations for his teaching. In that regard he shows a common interest with present-day teachers. As teachers today know, it is not enough to think about and plan what they will do in the course of a session. Their concern must also be for the learners and what changes will occur in them as a result of being in the session. Those changes are called learning outcomes.

Further, teachers know that they can't learn for their students. They can organize activities, establish good relationships, and create positive climates where learning can take place, but students must learn for themselves. A basic assumption for teachers is that, given appropriate relationships and activities, students are *able* to learn. There's not complete agreement on *how* that happens, but that it *does* happen is a basic premise of formal education.

Paul, I think, would have agreed that teachers need to be guided in their work by projected learning outcomes. And he would have supported the notion that teachers cannot learn for their students. But he would have taken that one step further. He insisted that what he was teaching could not be "learned," even by his students. The gospel, he claimed, was a revelation that could be received only by faith—and the faith to receive it was given only by the Holy Spirit. If Paul could not explain how people learn in general, he had strong convictions about how people came to believe in the Lord Jesus Christ. It was through the power of the Holy Spirit (1 Cor. 2:1ff.; 12:3; Rom. 8:9ff.).

This position is consistent with Paul's theological foundations: humankind, limited by sin, could not take the initiative leading to a reconciliation with God; in love, God acted in his Son to redeem the world; because of sin, faith in God's activity was not a human possibility, therefore, God had to create faith in the gospel in those Paul taught. And, not at all of secondary importance, Paul's theology on this point led back to his firm conviction that to God belongs all the glory.

There is something paradoxical about this aspect of Paul's teaching ministry. On the one hand, there is his theological stance described above. On the other hand, there is the practice of his ministry—his life's work. He was an indefatigable worker. He just never stopped—not in terms of his efforts to enlarge the understanding of those who had received the gospel, nor in his work to enlarge the number of those who heard it. In his own life and theology, Paul reflected the paradox he set before the Philippians when he wrote to them: ". . . work out your own salvation with fear and trembling; for God is at work in you, both to will and to work for his good pleasure" (Phil. 2:12-13). There's no resolving this paradox. There is no need to do so. We are left with Paul's insistence that God made possible the outcomes he hoped would follow as a result of his teaching. The most important of those outcomes, of course, was faith.

In at least three places in his letter to the Romans Paul reminded his readers of the purpose behind his making known the revelation of God in Christ. In Rom. 1:5 he wrote that it was from Christ he had received ". . . grace and apostleship to bring about the *obedience of faith* for the sake of his name among all the nations . . . ." Toward the end of the letter he repeated that purpose twice, concluding with the words:

> Now to him who is able to strengthen you according to my gospel and the preaching of Jesus Christ, according to the revelation of the mystery which was kept secret for long ages but is now disclosed and through the prophetic writings is made known to all nations, according to the command of the eternal God, to bring about the *obedience of faith* . . . (Rom. 16:25ff., emphasis added).

The phrase "obedience of faith" is a particularly rich one as a statement of purpose in Paul's teaching ministry. Most significantly, it reverses the order of the words that would suggest one could trust in obedience as the way of righteousness, that is, the faith of obedience. For Paul, obedience grew out of faith. He cited Abraham as the basis for his argument. Abraham, he wrote to the Romans, believed God, and because he believed God, he was able to be obedient to God's command to sacrifice his son, Isaac. As Paul suggests, this request of God's could not have made sense to the patriarch. It ran counter to the promise that Abraham would be the father of a great and numerous nation. Yet he trusted God. With this trust God was pleased.

Obedience, as Paul understood it, was a life lived in the Spirit and enabled by the Spirit. Nevertheless, it was obedience. In his proclamation of the gospel, Paul had no intention of surrendering that outcome. He had no more patience with those who used the gospel as an excuse for licentiousness than he did with the Judaizers who robbed the gospel of grace. His intent was to put obedience in its proper place—the response of one who, through faith, is living in a saving relationship with God, a relationship made possible by Christ. Obedience to Christ as Lord was, argued Paul, the vocation of the faithful.

Paul continuously challenged his congregations to live lives worthy of their calling in Jesus Christ (Rom. 12:1ff.). He didn't hesitate to point out what that life would include: holding fast the good, brotherly affection, prayer, generosity, patience, sensitivity to and meeting the needs of others, and forgiveness (Rom. 12:9ff.). Living in obedience to the faith also called for some capacity to prioritize convictions, especially when disputes arose within congregations. A case in point is the problem raised in Rome over the matter of eating food that had first been offered to idols. Noting first that one could, indeed, eat this food, Paul went on to say:

> Do not let what you eat cause the ruin of one for whom Christ died. So do not let your good be spoken of as evil. For the kingdom of God is not food and drink but righteousness and peace and joy in the Holy Spirit . . . . Let us then pursue what makes for peace and for mutual upbuilding. Do not, for the sake of food, destroy the work of God (Rom. 14:15ff.).

The concern in the passage above was for those who placed inordinate importance on winning arguments at the expense of hurting and losing people. Some arguments, of course, cannot be compromised—but not this one, said Paul. It's not easy to tell, but one wonders about other issues—some of which we face today—that Paul would have put in that same category. Might he not even be a bit chagrined to know that, in the minds of some, many of his opinions now have the force of law. How difficult it is to remember that his purpose was the response of obedience to the faith, and not simply obedience.

The purpose of obedience to the faith is one that runs through all of Paul's letters. In one of his most poignant passages Paul placed that purpose in the context of Jesus and his life of obedience. He wrote to the Philippians that Jesus, though he was in the form of God, emptied himself of that glory and was born in human flesh. Being born in the flesh, he further took the form of a servant, humbled himself, and became obedient unto death.

It was that mind, the mind of the obedient Jesus living in trustful relationship with God, that Paul hoped and prayed for in those he taught (Phil. 2:1ff.).

The Nurturing Purposes in Paul's Teaching

Once Paul had made known the revelation of the gospel and there had been a response of faith, he became concerned for another purpose in his teaching ministry—the growth and maturity of those he taught. While this was a challenge to his time and energy, it was something he couldn't ignore for at least two reasons. First, he saw it as a part of his responsibility as a teacher. Second, Paul recognized that obedience to the faith was a process of growing as well as an accomplished reality. These two reasons are interwoven in the discussion that follows.

In his letter to Titus, the apostle began: "Paul, a servant of God and an apostle of Jesus Christ, to further the faith of God's elect and their knowledge of the truth which accords with godliness . . ." (Titus 1:1). The furthering of the faith to which Paul referred had many dimensions. There was, for example, a need for Jews to recognize that Gentiles were included under God's grace. Gentiles, once they had received the gospel, had much to learn about God's activity in history and the nature of God's covenant with Israel. How faith was to become active in love was a matter of learning for both Jews and Gentiles. Paul had a keen sense of responsibility and, I think, of joy for making all this known.

Paul's purpose of helping others to grow is consistently reflected in his own activity. As a missionary he was a man on the move. Still he welcomed and sought opportunities where he could stay and teach. In several places, Corinth and Ephesus among them, Paul stayed for more than a year. During one such time, Acts reports, he was ". . . teaching the word of God among them" (Acts 18:11). On another occasion Paul wrote to the Corinthians that he couldn't come to them because in Ephesus ". . . a wide door for effective work has opened to me, and there are many adversaries" (1 Cor. 16:9). The presence of adversaries suggests that this, too, was a time for teaching. Paul also followed a pattern of returning to those congregations he had earlier established. These return visits must have been as much for the purpose of nurturing the young congregations as for adding people to their numbers.

Helping others to grow was not only a responsibility of his ministry to others, it was a concern of Paul's personal life as well. He wrote to the Philippians:

> Not that I have already obtained this or am already perfect; but I press on to make it my own, because Christ Jesus has made me his own. Brethren, I do not consider that I have made it my own; but one thing I do, forgetting what lies behind and straining forward to what lies ahead, I press on toward the goal for the prize of the upward call of God in Christ Jesus. Let those of us who are mature be thus minded . . . (Phil. 3:12-15a).

In this oft-quoted passage Paul noted several important ideas about growth. He described the direction it takes in the life of a believer. He also defined what he meant by maturity. For him, maturity didn't refer to a state or condition that would allow one to say: "I have arrived." It was quite the opposite. To be mature was to recognize that the journey of faith is open-ended. If anyone could have claimed that he had arrived at some lofty point of spiritual development, it would have been Paul. Yet, with all his insights, and in light of all that he had done, he saw the prize still out ahead of him.

Another notion that comes out in this text is that all who are mature are of the same mind as Paul—that is, they recognize their need to grow. This reflects Paul's definition of the teacher as an authority-enabler. As an authority, Paul was concerned for making the gospel known to others. That was the charge that had been given to him. In assisting the faithful to grow, and in having expectations for this growth, Paul was an enabler. These expectations are noted in several places in his letters.

Frequently Paul alluded to growth in the context of a compliment for the way in which a congregation had already grown. To the Thessalonians he wrote: "Finally, brethren, we beseech and exhort you in the Lord Jesus, that as you learned from us how you ought to live and to please God, just as you are doing, you do so more and more" (1 Thess. 4:1). Twice more in the letter Paul brought up the same theme (1 Thess. 4:10; 5:11). Apparently his letter had the desired effect, because he began his second letter by saying: "We are bound to give thanks to God always for you, brethren, as is fitting, because your faith is growing abundantly, and the love of every one of you for one another is increasing" (2 Thess. 1:3). In a similar way he wrote to the Philippians and Colossians (Phil. 1:9; Col. 1:6).

His letter to the Corinthians especially provides evidence that Paul also recognized problems and needs as stimuli for growth. For example, the offering for the saints in Jerusalem was an opportunity, Paul thought, for these people to grow in financial stewardship just as they had grown in other areas of their lives (2 Cor. 8:7). As this congregation grew, Paul saw it becoming a base for his continuing missionary work (2 Cor. 10:15-16). Not least, the many problems and questions that developed at Corinth led him to pray, perhaps with a sigh, that these people would sometime improve (2 Cor. 13:9).

The references above suggest that there was both a personal and a corporate dimension to Paul's concern for growth. While the relationship between the two is implicit in what Paul wrote, a few comments here could bring into sharper perspective their mutual interdependence. As Paul pointed out in 1 Corinthians 9, he spent his life in an effort to persuade others of the truth of the gospel and in calling for the response of faith. He was willing to identify with each person he met—whether Jew or Greek, male or female, rich or poor—in order to "win" them for the gospel. Paul's approach, whether speaking to a group of Jews in a synagogue or to a single person such as Lydia, was intensely personal.

Still, his teaching had a corporate dimension as well. One should expect that of Paul, for Paul was a Jew. Individual identity and self-understanding arose for the Jews out of the context of their community. As noted in the Introduction, one reason the Jews established schools was for the purpose of sustaining that identity in the young, in order that the community of Israel might be continued. The individual, the community, and their shared heritage together made Israel. Paul didn't depart from this notion when he envisioned the church as a body. Each part of the body, he wrote to the Romans, had its own function. But all the parts of the body depend upon the whole for life and growth (Rom. 12:4ff.). As individuals grew, the church was strengthened. As the church grew, it became better able to help its members to grow. Outside of this interdependence, cemented together by a common faith and heritage, neither individuals nor congregations could grow.

Having considered Paul's overall purposes of faith and growth, what remains now is to examine in a somewhat more specific way the purposes that guided Paul's teaching. Rather than attempt to do so through a careful analysis of each of his letters, I've chosen to summarize his purposes in three categories familiar to teachers today: the cognitive, the affective, and the behavioral. In this overview of Paul's letters it needs to be remembered that these letters are responses to issues and questions that arose as a result of his earlier preaching and teaching. As such, they do not necessarily represent the teaching strategy that guided Paul when he first came to places like Corinth or Thessalonica. Except for some speeches in Acts, we simply don't know how Paul presented his material to his learners—or the purposes that would have prompted his choice of material and approach. What we have in his letters may be compared to a discussion period that follows a teacher's presentation. As teachers know, the discussion phase of a class can go off in almost any direction and may or may not address the crucial issues raised by the teacher.

There must be some of that peripheral material in Paul's letters, especially as he was asked to comment on issues that arose in one or another of his congregations. As Pinchas Lapide suggests, it's not likely that it was Paul's purpose to limit the role of all women in the church to silence simply because there were a few women in the Corinthian congregation who couldn't keep quiet during the worship service.[1] Yet, in the broad outlines of his epistles, there are consistent themes that must be taken as representative of Paul's purposes in his teaching. The very fact that these discussions take the shape of letters rather than spontaneous conversation indicates that Paul allowed himself time to give careful thought as to what he wanted to say and how he wanted to say it. Given that allowance, it's clear that Paul consistently pulled his thoughts together around the one great theme (purpose) he was convinced he was called to preach and teach—Jesus Christ, and him crucified (1 Cor. 2:2).

Dimensions of the Teaching Purposes of Paul

While not always aware of it, various members of congregations today frequently express themselves on the matter of the purpose of the educational program they support. For example, I've heard parents say something like this: "Why don't our kids learn something in confirmation classes these days? When I was in confirmation I had to memorize the Catechism and study the Bible." In an education class for first-year seminarians, one student argued: "I think there's altogether too much emphasis on information in church school classes. I intend to put a lot more stress

---

[1]Pinchas Lapide and Peter Stuhlmacher, *Paul: Rabbi and Apostle* (Minneapolis: Augsburg, 1984) pp. 35-36.

on relationships when I teach." Still others have been heard to
say: "There's altogether too much talk about religion amongst
members of the church. What Christians need is a lot less talk
and a lot more action."

When comments like these are made by teachers they are particularly revealing, because they represent varied priorities that
are likely to be present in every congregation's church school.
Some teachers place a high priority on learning information, and
their expectations of students and how they teach reflect that
priority. Others are more concerned for the attitudes and relationships that are developed in the church school. And there are
those teachers who are primarily concerned for the behavior of
those they teach. Educators translate those three priorities into
statements of purpose and give each a name. Those that primarily
relate to information and the use of information are called *cognitive*
purposes. The ones that emphasize values, attitudes, and feelings
are called *affective* purposes. The ones that concentrate on how
learners are to act are referred to as *behavioral,* or performance,
purposes.

These three categories of educational purpose reflect three dimensions of human life—the mind, the heart, and the body.
While these distinct dimensions exist, there is little argument
that both teachers and learners function wholistically. That is,
humans have feelings about what they know, and what they know
and feel influences what they do. In a way, these three form a
triad—wherever one is present, the other two are sure to be
present as well.

As the statements above indicate, however, there is the possibility in formal education to emphasize one or the other. That
may be appropriate for a particular class session. But when that
emphasis is maintained over the course of many sessions, or becomes the central focus of a teacher's way of being with learners,
there can be negative consequences. Among those consequences

is the possibility of the learner's failure to gain a wholistic understanding of what it means to be a person—a Christian person.

Balance in the Educational Purposes of Paul

If contemporary educators have given names to three dimensions of educational purpose, they certainly didn't invent those categories. The apostle Paul was very much aware of them. Indeed, it's possible to understand many of the controversies in which he was engaged as arguments over the relative importance of the cognitive, the affective, and the behavioral in the life and education of the Christian. As the history of the church has evolved, the struggle over the relationship of the three in its theology has remained a central issue for debate, with the age of pietism reflecting a preoccupation with the affective and the age of rationalism demonstrating a commitment to the cognitive.

By selectively quoting from his letters, one can enlist Paul as an advocate for emphasizing any one of the three dimensions. The very fact that this possibility exists suggests that Paul's teaching purposes have to be seen as decidedly wholistic. That is not to say, necessarily, that he devoted equal amounts of space in his letters to each of the three dimensions. What is meant is that Paul did not allow for the exclusion, or even the de-emphasis, of any of those dimensions. In the following I have drawn attention to places in his letters that stress one or the other of them. My purpose in doing so is not to suggest that Paul dealt with them as separate entities but rather, because he included all three, that he would have argued that they are, as purposes for teaching, inseparable.

The Behavioral Dimension in Paul's Teaching Purposes

There's an irony in how Paul's letters are read with respect to the behavioral dimension of his teaching purposes. Some, perhaps fearful of compromising "justification by grace through faith" and/or the Christian's freedom in the gospel, relegate this to a position of relative unimportance in Paul's teaching. At the other extreme, whole church bodies attempt to govern themselves by Paul's comments about what is appropriate behavior for Christians.

While careful not to surrender the gospel, Paul was tremendously concerned for the behavior of those who confessed Jesus as Lord. As free as Christians were, their behavior was to communicate to others, among other things: goodness, kindness, gentleness, and self-control (Gal. 5:22ff.). Further, the behavior of Christians was to reflect the transformation that God had wrought in them through Baptism. Grace, wrote Paul, was not a license for the Romans to continue in sin, but a power to live lives worthy of their calling in Jesus Christ (Rom. 6:1ff.; 12:1ff.). Where behavior, such as eating food offered first to idols, had no direct effect on the person doing the act, Paul still called upon the members of the Roman congregation to weigh the import of their actions. If their doing had a negative effect on others, Paul recommended a change in behavior (Rom. 14:13ff).

Hearing of some of their problems, Paul admonished persons in Corinth to cease their immoral actions, whatever they might be. He called upon husbands and wives to demonstrate their love for each other and for parents and children to show mutual respect. He criticized the same congregation for the way they behaved when they celebrated the Lord's Supper and scorned their cliques. The Romans were encouraged to behave in ways that demonstrated their hospitality, their empathy for each other, and their mutual respect. He assumed that members of this congregation would contribute to the needs of the saints, recognize the authority of the state by paying their taxes, and use the gifts God had given by praying, singing, teaching, evangelizing, healing, and administrating the church. All these verbs describe behavior

that was reflective of a Christian life-style. Paul provided an overall context for those verbs when he wrote to the Philippians:

> Finally, brethren, whatever is true, whatever is honorable, what-
> ever is just, whatever is pure, whatever is lovely, whatever is gra-
> cious, if there is any excellence, if there is anything worthy of
> praise, think about these things. What you have learned and re-
> ceived and heard and seen in me, do . . . (Phil. 4:8-9).

While it can be argued, and appropriately so, that Paul's behavioral expectations of his learners were open-ended, they are
not without some structure and definition. The references above
illustrate that a part of his purpose in teaching was to provide
that structure for his congregations. Further behavioral expectations will become evident as the cognitive and affective dimensions of his teaching are discussed.

The Cognitive Dimension in Paul's Teaching
Purposes

However one describes Paul's ministry, the one purpose di-
recting all that he did was that of making known to others God's
gracious act in Jesus Christ. Until the gospel was known, the
response of faith was not possible. Paul put it succinctly when
he wrote to the Romans:

> But how are men to call upon him in whom they have not
> believed? And how are they to believe in him of whom they have
> never heard? And how are they to hear without a preacher? (Rom.
> 10:14).

The answer to Paul's questions was simply that someone had to
make the gospel known to others, and that is a purpose within
the cognitive realm. Once the gospel was made known, it was
Paul's purpose to enlarge the context out of which it came and

to deepen the understanding of it among those who received it in faith. Those, too, are purposes that can be rightly identified as cognitive.

Some years ago Benjamin Bloom described several levels of cognitive thinking that provide a useful framework to discuss Paul's teaching purposes. Moving from the least to the most complex, those levels are:

Memory—recalling data (information).

Comprehension—demonstrating an understanding of the data by translating it into another form.

Application—using information in some way, i.e., to solve a problem or suggest a course of action.

Analysis—examining a story, problem, situation, or text in terms of its parts.

Synthesis—drawing the analyzed parts back into a new whole.

Evaluation—developing and applying criteria for determining effectiveness and purpose.[2]

Paul, of course, didn't have the benefit of Bloom's research by which to determine if his purposes incorporated more than, say, the memory level. Apparently he didn't need it, for examples of all these levels can be found in his letters. It would go beyond my purpose here to explore in detail all of Paul's letters in search of those examples. An overview of one, that to the Galatians, should be adequate to illustrate my point.

The information level.   A fair amount of the introductory material in Galatians is data—autobiographical information concerning the apostle's call and the early developments in his ministry. He reminded his readers that, among other things, he had been a zealous student of the traditions of his fathers, that he had

---

[2]Benjamin S. Bloom, ed., *Taxonomy of Educational Objectives* (White Plains, N.Y.: Longman, 1956), pp. 62-200.

persecuted the church, that he had received a revelation of Jesus, that the gospel he preached was consistent with that of the leaders of the church in Jerusalem, and that at least on one occasion he had stood up to Peter with regard to pressures brought to bear on Paul's understanding of the gospel. Enlarging on that spare outline, one could construct a biography of its author.

But of what value is this information? Why did Paul choose to place it here in his introduction to the letter to the Galatians? What purpose does it have for readers today? Requiring students to simply memorize data such as this is, I think, what gives a bad impression of cognitive purposes in religious education. Of course, the data is necessary, but what makes it interesting is to discover why Paul wrote these details in this particular letter, and to do that requires one to deal with evaluative thinking.

The evaluative level.   The evaluative level, it will be remembered, has to do with generating and using evaluative criteria. In the early church, one of the criteria for apostleship was that the person be instructed and commissioned by the Lord Jesus. Paul could not meet this criterion in the same way that Peter and others of the disciples did. Unable to do so, his authority as a teacher, his very apostleship, was open to challenge.

In the autobiographical data Paul gave, however, he pointed out that he, too, had been commissioned by Jesus. He had received a revelation of the Lord, and through that revelation his life had been transformed. Acknowledging the church's criteria for apostleship, Paul set his life before his readers and asked them to evaluate the legitimacy of his ministry, confident that his claims would be recognized. In doing so, Paul was taking great risks, not least the risk that his readers could and would do evaluative thinking and then, having done so, could affirm his authority as a teacher.

The analysis level.   The Scriptures for Paul were the books of the Old Testament. When he asked his readers to analyze a text, it was an Old Testament one to which he referred. He did this several times in his letter to the Galatians. He took for granted that these people knew the stories of Abraham and Moses and how they fit into the overall history of Israel. Through Abraham, he reminded them, came the covenant of promise that had been received through faith. Four hundred years later God gave the law through Moses. Note the order, wrote Paul. The covenant of promise came first, and that covenant had never been set aside. The law hadn't established the relationship between God and Israel; it had been added for the purpose of serving as a custodian for those living in the promise of God.

The application level.   Once his readers had more carefully analyzed the basis for Israel's relationship with God, Paul asked them to apply that understanding to God's revelation in Jesus Christ as it related to the Gentiles. God's gift in Christ, Paul argued, was to extend the covenant of promise to all that all, both Jews and Gentiles, apart from the law, might know his grace. The manner in which God initiated the relationship with the Gentiles was consistent with that of Israel. Again, since it was God's act, it was to be received by faith—apart from any works of the law, even that of circumcision. Applying all this to Baptism, Paul wrote:

> For as many of you as were baptized into Christ have put on Christ. There is neither Jew nor Greek, there is neither slave nor free, there is neither male nor female; for you are all one in Christ Jesus. And if you are Christ's, then you are Abraham's offspring, heirs according to promise (Gal. 3:27ff.).

The synthesis level.   The entire letter to the Galatians represents a synthesis in Paul's thinking that he endeavored to communicate to others. That synthesis didn't happen quickly, though the content for it was all pretty much in place immediately following his Damascus road experience. In his autobiographical statements Paul alluded to some time spent alone—or at least apart from the church in Jerusalem. During that time Paul must have done a considerable amount of reflection, attempting to understand how the revelation he had received fit in with what he had been taught by Gamaliel. What came out of that reflection was a new, or enlarged, appreciation of how God relates to his creation. Paul was to conclude that the revelation of God was always to center on grace, and the center of that grace was Jesus Christ.

As an example of that synthesis, Paul asked his readers to consider the relationship of Hagar and Sarah and their sons with Abraham. Hagar and her son, he contended, represented the law and slavery. The promise of grace was not with them. Isaac, on the other hand, was the promised child of Sarah and Abraham. He is the example of one who lives in the freedom that God freely bestows through his grace and favor, apart from works of the law. The inheritance—living in God's favor—is God's alone to give. That favor, said Paul, is for all those who receive it in faith in the saving act of Jesus Christ. This synthesis, developing out of the roots of Israel's heritage as the chosen people of God and understood in the light of the death and resurrection of Jesus, was Paul's gift to the church, a gift that he was confident had its origin in God. That synthesis remains at the center of the church's confession of faith and provides, along with the gospels, the core of the criteria for determining that which is truly Christian.

The comprehension level.   Much of Galatians reflects Paul's anger that these people had not really comprehended what he had previously taught them. Hardly into the letter he expressed his astonishment that they were allowing themselves to be influenced by "a different gospel." If they had understood what he had taught, did they really think that there could be two gospels? At another point he calls them "foolish Galatians." Their foolishness was found in their failure to comprehend the true nature of the gospel and how its promises became true in their lives. Their confusion about what constituted the gospel, a problem of comprehension, provided the occasion for Paul's letter.

In the foregoing I have attempted to illustrate that Paul's teaching purposes included the full range of the cognitive levels of thinking. It would be a mistake, however, to conclude that Paul did this consciously—that he intentionally worked at this inclusion in a structured sort of way or moved deliberately from one level to another. On the contrary, the material taken from Galatians shows that these levels are as interrelated and dependent on each other in Paul's teaching as are the dimensions of the cognitive, affective, and behavioral—and that it would not have occurred to him to separate them. In his letter to the Corinthians, however, Paul does express an awareness of different levels of some sort. It's not clear, when he writes that he had to give these people milk rather than solid food, that he was referring to their inability to think on a complex level (1 Cor. 3:1ff.). That may have been part of it, but the context suggests that there was something beyond cognitive thinking that the Corinthians lacked—and that was spiritual insight. That leads into one last observation before leaving this discussion of cognitive purposes in Paul's teaching.

As noted earlier, Paul's teaching purpose did not end with making the gospel known. He also looked for the response of faith. Struggling with the issue of when knowledge becomes faith, and how that occurs, is one of the tasks of Christian theology. In this context it needs to be said that the transition from knowledge to faith cannot be identified with any particular level of cognitive thinking. The ability to work with the biblical story from both ends of the cognitive continuum doesn't guarantee that a person has faith in what is known. At the same time, the inability to think on any given level is no evidence that faith is lacking.

What is faith? Though it occupied a central place in his theology, Paul didn't really define it. Others have attempted to do so. Early in its history the church taught that faith had three parts: knowledge, assent to knowledge, and trust. James Fowler claims that faith is that on which we are willing to stake our lives. The writer of Hebrews wrote that faith is: ". . . the assurance of things hoped for, the conviction of things not seen" (Heb. 11:1). A colleague of mine says it is "acting on what we know." Martin Luther wrote:

> Faith is the yes of the heart, a conviction on which one stakes one's life. On what does faith rest? On Christ, born of a woman, made under the law, who died etc., as the children pray. To this confession I say yes with the full confidence of my heart. Christ came for my sake, in order to set me free from the law, not only from the guilt of sin but also from the power of the law. If you are able to say yes to this, you have what is called faith; and this faith does every thing. . . . But this faith does not grow by our own powers. On the contrary, the Holy Spirit is present and writes it in the heart.[3]

A gift of God, centered in Jesus Christ, on which a person stakes his or her life seems to be what is meant when the church speaks of faith. Where there is faith, there is more than knowledge about Jesus: there is the confession that Jesus is Lord. While that definition doesn't eliminate the mystery inherent to the whole notion of faith, it does make clear that it incorporates the affective as well as the cognitive and behavioral dimensions.

---

[3]Ewald M. Plass, ed., *What Luther Says,* vol. 1 (St. Louis: Concordia, 1959), pp. 466-67.

The Affective Dimension in Paul's Teaching Purposes

I once overheard the remark: "I hate the word 'feeling.' Feelings continuously distort the Christian faith." Without a doubt, feelings are a powerful force that, once unleashed, can bring havoc to the faith of persons, congregations, and church bodies. As volatile as they may be, however, they are a significant part of everyone's life—not least a Christian's. As such, Paul didn't hesitate to address them, and the whole realm of the affective, in his purposes for teaching. David Krathwahl has described a taxonomy of educational purposes for the affective realm much as Benjamin Bloom did for the cognitive. Rather than use that taxonomy here as a structure for this discussion, I have chosen to consider several aspects of the affective dimension as they are reflected in the letters of Paul. Those aspects are: values, relationships, and attitudes and feelings.

Relationships in the teaching purposes of Paul.   If Paul wasn't a favorite with all the people he met, he did establish many close connections. The people with whom he shared his ministry are among the most noteworthy of his friends. The names of Silas, Timothy, Luke, and Barnabas are familiar to readers of the New Testament—primarily because of their friendship with Paul. Though Paul and Barnabas had a falling-out over John Mark's qualifications for ministry, it's a tribute to both men that they were able to work out a reconciliation. Paul's capacity for teamwork and his willingness to adopt that approach in his ministry suggests that this was a model he commended to the church. Further, his analogy of the church as a body with many members, all necessary for the well-being of the whole, indicates the importance he placed on relationships in the life and growth of the church.

Not a few of the problems he addressed in his letters had to do with relationships. The problem with respect to the celebration of the Lord's Supper in Corinth is a case in point. By allowing the supper to become an occasion for some to flaunt their wealth or for others to turn it into some sort of revelry, the attitudes of reverence and an appropriate sense of equality among all participants were being destroyed. While Paul's exhortation that those who eat and drink at the table must discern the body of Christ has been variously interpreted, at least one understanding is that Paul was reminding the Corinthians that they were to acknowledge the fellowship of one another as they shared in the sacrament (1 Cor. 11:17ff.).

Paul's thoughts on the Lord's Supper are followed immediately by his description of the church as a body with many members. Both serve as a preamble to Paul's great hymn of love, 1 Corinthians 13, in which he presents the more excellent way by which people can live together. Paul's letters are full of advice on how to develop and maintain relationships. He encouraged the Romans to avoid any pompous notions about their own importance. Rather, they were to ". . . love one another with brotherly affection; outdo[ing] one another in showing honor" (Rom. 12:3, 10). Whatever they did, they were to ". . . pursue what makes for peace and for mutual upbuilding" (Rom. 14:19). Among the qualities important to that end was hospitality.

I think Paul was aware that it wasn't necessarily possible to like everyone and that living in Christian communities was not easy. There were some who would be difficult to relate to. They, too, however, were to be admitted and helped in the fellowship of faith. Paul wrote: "We who are strong ought to bear with the failings of the weak, and not to please ourselves; let each of us please his neighbor for his good, to edify him" (Rom. 15:1-2). Continuing along those same lines, Paul gave his reason for the believer's concern for relationships with others. He wrote: "Welcome one another, therefore, as Christ has welcomed you, for the glory of God" (Rom. 15:7).

For Paul, Christ's coming was for the purpose of restoring the relationship between God and humankind. Whatever the facts of the story, what the gospel meant was that God, in Christ, had reconciled the world unto himself (2 Cor. 5:18). For Christ's sake the Gentile world was welcomed into the family of God. As Paul noted in his letter to the Romans, that welcome was extended to people who were far less than perfect (Rom. 5:6). Ought they not, then, in the name of Christ, include others, different though they may be, in the fellowship of the church?

Paul not only wrote about relationships and experienced good ones with his coworkers, he also established many relationships in the communities where he taught and preached. The closing lines of Romans read like the membership rolls of a congregation—name after name of persons to whom Paul sent his personal greetings. The letters to the Philippians and Colossians also contain many references that indicate his closeness to particular persons. His departure from Ephesus, on his way to Jerusalem, is a clear indication of the love and respect others had for the apostle. The writer of Acts described that parting in this way:

> And when he [Paul] had spoken thus, he knelt down and prayed with them all. And they all wept and embraced Paul and kissed him, sorrowing most of all because of the word he had spoken, that they should see his face no more (Acts 20:36-38).

Even in those personal references in his letters to the Galatians and Corinthians which are less than warm, his intent seems to have been that of restoring a sound basis for relationship. Those who created disharmony in the church, either by their false teaching or their inappropriate behavior, could expect to hear from Paul. While the apostle was not adverse to asking people to leave the fellowship if they continued in their disruptive ways, his hope and intent was always to retain the unity of the church.

I wonder if Paul might not think it odd that teachers in the church today would have to make arguments in defense of the relational purposes of their teaching. Those purposes were so much a part of Paul's teaching that any description of what he did would be incomplete without them. After all, at the center of his theology was the message that God had restored the broken relationship with his creation. At the center of his work was the establishment of congregations—groups of people living together in the fellowship of the gospel.

Values in the teaching purposes of Paul.   There isn't much in Paul's letters that doesn't in some way reflect the values that informed and directed his own life and that he taught to others. Therefore, again, only a brief overview of some of those values can be given here to illustrate that these, too, had a place in the overall purposes of Paul's teaching ministry.

Paul valued persons and the freedom they had been given in Christ. When the Judaizers attempted to bring in the law as a precondition for fellowship in the church at Galatia, Paul responded with a resounding no. Their worth, Paul argued, was founded on nothing less than God's favor, and the law could add nothing to that. Having been set free, Paul admonished them not to allow themselves to be enslaved to the law, or anything else, again. Yet the freedom they had was to be used responsibly. One guideline for its responsible use was that of recognizing the value of other persons. If others were led to stumble because of what a believer did, that behavior should be surrendered for the sake of the other (Rom. 14:13ff.).

The worth of persons in the church was not a factor of their office, intelligence, or connections. No, it was not even a reflection of the depth of their faith (Rom. 12:3). God, in the gift of his Son, had revealed the worth of his creation in the price he had paid to redeem it. No one shared in that highest of estimates except by the favor of God, and thus none could claim a higher value than another (2 Cor. 5:16ff.).

Again Paul demonstrated his grasp of realities when he acknowledged that, in terms of human estimates, all people don't seem to be of equal value. In his letters to both the Corinthians and the Romans, Paul urged his readers not to be deluded by those appearances and directed their attention to the image of the body that needed the coordination of all of its parts in order for the whole to function effectively (Rom. 12:4ff.; 1 Cor. 12:1ff.). Because Paul valued all persons, he encouraged the doing of those things that led to solid relationships, as described in the previous section.

Paul valued the human body. Paul was not one to separate the body from the spirit. Misuse of the body was, for Paul, no more excusable than a wrong understanding of the gospel. He wrote to the Corinthians: "Do you not know that your body is a temple of the Holy Spirit within you, which you have from God? You are not your own; you were bought with a price. So glorify God in your body" (1 Cor. 6:19-20). While it may be stretching it to say that Paul was an advocate of athletics, there's no doubt that he disciplined his own body and made it serve his purposes. At the same time he censured those who misused their bodies—whether that was done through drunkenness, sexual immorality, or anything else. His objections, as already noted, weren't just a matter of personal preference. He valued the body as the temple of the Spirit. Anything that detracted from that value was unacceptable to him.

Paul valued work. Paul's life as a missionary is evidence of his great capacity for, and commitment to, work. But Paul was not content to let his service in the gospel stand as his sole work. He was determined to earn what he needed to sustain himself by means of some sort of productive work in addition to what he did as preacher and teacher. He had the same expectations of others, as he made known in his letter to the Thessalonians:

Now we command you, brethren, in the name of our Lord Jesus Christ, that you keep away from any brother who is living in idleness and not in accordance with the tradition that you received from us. For you yourselves know how you ought to imitate us; we were not idle when we were with you, we did not eat anyone's bread without paying, but with toil and labor we worked night and day, that we might not burden any of you. It was not because we have not that right, but to give you in our conduct an example to imitate. For even when we were with you, we gave you this command: If any one will not work, let him not eat (2 Thess. 3:6-10).

It's no wonder that ordained pastors who earn some or all of their income apart from the contributions of their congregations are called tentmakers—the work of the apostle Paul.

Paul valued the Word. The written Word for Paul was the Old Testament. That Word was considered by him as authoritative. He began his presentations, according to Acts, with recitations of the story of Israel found in those Scriptures. His proclamation of Jesus as Messiah was anchored in his reading of the Old Testament. His illustrations used to clarify his teachings were invariably taken from the same source. And the evidence he used to buttress his arguments on most any issue came from those same Scriptures.

The word Paul valued, however, extended beyond what we know as the Old Testament. The word he heard on the Damascus road was determinative for him and his ministry. The word that he heard on the lips of the martyred Stephen, and repeated again and again among the followers of Jesus gathered for worship, had authority for Paul. Jesus was, for Paul, God's most gracious and clear Word. It was for that Word that Paul gave himself.

Paul valued integrity. The apostle Paul had a singleness of vision to which he was so committed that he often found himself in difficulty with others who couldn't, or hadn't, reached the same level of integration in their lives. That integrity made it simply impossible for Paul to negotiate on matters of the gospel, and it brought him into conflict with Cephas (Peter) at Antioch when the disciple bent to the demands of the circumcision party (Gal. 2:11ff.). Before a crowd in Jerusalem threatening to take his life, that same integrity led him to request one more opportunity to speak the gospel. The consequence of that sermon was that his life was even more seriously threatened. Integrity must have been a quality that he sensed in himself—an integrity that bound together his words with his actions. What else could justify his claim that others would do well to imitate him?

Those included above are not intended to represent a complete catalog of all that Paul valued. Many of his values have been noted in other places—faith, prayer, love, the church; the list could go on and on. One other, however, should be noted before concluding this discussion—that of marriage. Paul's understanding of marriage, and especially the role of women in marriage, has been a matter of some debate. There are passages, such as 1 Cor. 7:1ff., where Paul seemed to see marriage as primarily a safe arena in which to find sexual gratification. In the same chapter he recommended that those who weren't already married should stay as they were. To a large degree that suggestion arose out of his expectation that the end times would soon be upon them, but there was more to it than that. Paul seemed to see marriage as a source of anxiety—an anxiety about worldly things that detracted from one's concentration on the "affairs of the Lord."

From one perspective this is a rather negative view of the marriage relationship. Yet, if one changes perspective, the view isn't necessarily so negative. To begin with, it must be acknowledged that Paul called for equality and sensitivity in marriage, especially in the matter of sexual relations between husbands and wives (1 Cor. 7:3-5). And his realistic acceptance of a husband's and wife's concern for the other, and together for their children, legitimizes that concern where it exists. Paul assumed that the family would be a high priority for parents. If he chose not to marry, that didn't mean others shouldn't, or that the responsibilities of marriage were not important. On the contrary, they were to be taken very seriously. Finally, it's doubtful if Paul would have used the image of marriage as an analogy for Christ's relationship with the church—as a bridegroom to a bride—if he had not valued that image.

If the subject of Paul's values has not been exhausted in the above, enough has been noted to demonstrate that this aspect of the affective dimension was extremely important in his teaching. Having done so, I think it's safe to say that Paul would not have understood any attempt to make teaching value-free, or the notion that teachers ought not try to influence the values of those they teach. Paul was the type of teacher who made it a point to inculcate in his students those values that he saw as arising out of the gospel—and he did it with no apologies.

Feelings and attitudes in the teaching purposes of Paul. When it comes to separating feelings from values and relationships, one becomes aware of how impossible a task this is. Still, there are some purposes in the teaching of Paul that I have reserved for this section, aware that they might have been included in other sections of this chapter as well.

Feelings, of course, refer to our emotions. Or, if you prefer, reflect the dispositions of our hearts. Words like *joy, sadness, anger, gladness, sorrow, praise, awe, thanksgiving, hope,* and *love* are among those we use to describe how we "feel." Paul used those words, too, and took account of the feelings they represented in the personal and corporate lives of those he taught. Try, for example, to imagine his letter to the Philippians without the context of joy in which it was written. Ignore the anger spread all over the letter to the Galatians, and one is left with a theological debate without any passion for truth or for people. A not-so-subtle indignation runs through Paul's letters to the Corinthians—a deep hurt that his teaching, his work, and his authority could be so misunderstood and undervalued by these people.

Paul, chief of sinners that he was, didn't lack for self-esteem. He never forgot that in his early years he was at the head of the class in his study of the Judaic traditions. As a servant of the church he claimed parity with the pillars in Jerusalem and could provide a resumé of experiences that few could match for daring, adventure, and suffering (2 Cor. 11:1ff.) At the same time, Paul could admit to sorrow over the people of Israel (Rom. 9:2), anxiety for the churches (2 Cor. 11:28), and the need for a thorn in the flesh to curb his own elation (2 Cor. 12:7ff.).

Doxologies—expressions of joy, awe, and thanksgiving—are scattered throughout Paul's letters. Whatever else these are, they are expressions of the disposition of Paul's heart. Concluding his discussion of the resurrection in 1 Corinthians, Paul exploded with the phrase: "But thanks be to God, who gives us the victory through our Lord Jesus Christ" (15:57). Recognizing that after all he had written in his letter to the Romans, he hadn't really explained the mystery of God's love in Jesus, Paul finally admitted:

> O the depth of the riches and wisdom and knowledge of God! How unsearchable are his judgments and how inscrutable his ways! "For who has known the mind of the Lord, or who has been his counselor?" "Or who has given a gift to him that he might be repaid?" For from him and through him and to him are all things. To him be glory forever. Amen (Rom. 11:33-36).

Paul was a person of deep feelings who made little effort to conceal them—whether anger, joy, sorrow, indignation, affection, awe, praise, or peace. Knowing the power of the emotions, Paul commended the more obviously positive ones in his teaching as ways of entering more profoundly into the life situations of others and of experiencing more significantly a relationship with God. And I suspect he may have justified his feelings of anger as righteous indignation. However angry he became, he refused to cut himself off from those he claimed to be his own—even when he said that he would. Congregations today that have trouble confronting issues and differences of opinion could learn from Paul, a teacher who didn't go directly from conflict to separation.

A Summary of Paul's Teaching Purposes

It's been mentioned several times throughout this chapter that the only way to do an exhaustive analysis of Paul's teaching purposes would be to write a commentary on each of his epistles from the point of view of educational objectives. That has not been my purpose in this chapter. Rather I have attempted to show the inclusiveness of Paul's teaching purposes by using categories familiar to teachers today. I have chosen material from Paul's letters and Acts to illustrate my points. Undoubtedly I have not included all that could be said concerning the purposes of Paul's teaching. It is hoped I have provided enough to support the argument that the gospel was at the center of what he taught, and that it gave direction to everything else he taught—cognitive, affective, and behavioral.

For Reflection

1. If you are a teacher, what is the central purpose(s) that guide you in your teaching?
2. What part do the cognitive, affective, and behavioral dimensions have in your teaching?
3. How clear do you think the church is today about its purpose(s) for the teaching/learning ministry it supports?
4. In what ways are the purposes for Christian religious education similar/different from those of Paul described in this chapter? What, in your opinion, accounts for those similarities and differences?

CHAPTER FOUR ====

PAUL'S ACCOUNTABILITY IN TEACHING

In the Introduction to this study the claim was made that teaching was an important dimension in the overall ministry of Paul. Further, it has been said that he was a teacher of a particular kind, with specific purposes and certain understandings of himself and those he taught. All these converge at a point I've chosen to call accountability.

Though accountability may be a somewhat new word in the vocabulary of teachers, it's a concept with a long history. There have always been expectations of teachers. How, and the degree to which, teachers responded to these expectations determined the measure of their accountability. A few generations ago those expectations were most often expressed in terms of performance and life-style. While these remain, at least in some places, there has developed a growing expectation that students show favorable progress in their learning as a result of their association with a teacher. That is, teachers are no longer just responsible for their own behavior, but for being able to demonstrate some positive change in those they teach.

Although some teachers seem to fear the notion of accountability and may even see it as an infringement upon their freedom, it is not a bad thing. It can be, of course, if the expectations upon which the accountability is based are inappropriate and/or distorted. But simply because there have been times and places where expectations have been abused is no reason to abandon them, or the notion of accountability.

There are many levels on which accountability is experienced. It comes, for example, to students in the form of tests, papers, or tasks that are designed to measure whether or not they have achieved the objectives for a particular learning experience. Those same forms reflect back upon the teacher and provide a basis for measuring whether students have been taught in such a way that they have been assisted in their learning.

Tests and papers aren't, of course, the only ways to get at the matter of accountability. Unhappiness with them has led some teachers to dispense with the whole notion of accountability—as if they could. However, like it or not, accountability is present in every teaching/learning situation. What is needed is a clear expression of existing expectations and how persons in a given situation are to be held accountable for them.

While it is necessary to have some objective, outside-the-person means for determining accountability, in the end it is a quality teachers have to carry within themselves. Without commitment—and its counterpart, accountability—toward what they are about in the lives of those they teach, one can't be a teacher. The apostle Paul had that commitment, and for that reason, if for no other, he can be described as a teacher. For him there were at least three areas in which he demonstrated accountability: first, to himself and his calling; second, to the material that he taught; and third, to the ones he taught. These in turn were shaped by his definition of teachers and learners and by the purposes that brought them together.

Paul's Accountability to Himself

At first glance it would seem that Paul wasn't much interested in the whole matter of accountability—at least with respect to himself. He wrote to the Corinthians: "But with me it is a very small thing that I should be judged by you or any human court. I do not even judge myself. . ." (1 Cor. 4:3). If Paul was not much concerned for how others might measure him, he more than made up for it in his own self-awareness—of who he was and what he was called to do. Each time he began a letter, he reminded his readers that he was a servant of Jesus Christ. In several of his letters he stated the credentials that authenticated him as an apostle of Christ, and he also expressed to whom and to what he was accountable—to Jesus Christ and the gospel. With respect to that, Paul wrote to the Corinthians: "This is how one should regard us, as servants of Christ and stewards of the mysteries of God. Moreover it is required of stewards that they be found trustworthy" (1 Cor. 4:1-2).

Being accountable to the gospel gave Paul an amazing degree of freedom. Again he wrote to the Corinthians:

> For though I am free from all men, I have made myself a slave to all, that I might win the more. To the Jews I became as a Jew, in order to win Jews; to those under the law I became as one under the law—though not being myself under the law—that I might win those under the law. To those outside the law I became as one outside the law—not being without law toward God but under the law of Christ—that I might win those outside the law. To the weak I became weak, that I might win the weak. I have become all things to all men, that I might by all means save some. I do it all for the sake of the gospel, that I may share in its blessing (1 Cor. 9:19ff.).

Paul went on to say that he did all this with intensity and a sense of purpose, not just for the sake of doing it. Like an athlete training to win a race, Paul lived and carried out his ministry.

Becoming all things to others in order to win them for Christ describes one side of Paul's personal sense of accountability. The other is summarized in his letter to the Galatians: "I have been crucified with Christ; it is no longer I who live, but Christ who lives in me; and the life I now live in the flesh I live by faith in the Son of God, who loved me and gave himself for me" (Gal. 2:20). To be sure, he made no claim to perfection. He had a keen awareness that his life with Christ was leading him somewhere. At the same time, however, the Lord of his life had become so much a part of his life that Paul would not have wanted to separate the two. Within him Christ dwelled, and to that Christ within him he was accountable.

Confident that he had been called to be an ambassador for Christ, he took the gospel wherever he could, establishing congregations in which Jesus was confessed as Lord. Profoundly aware that he had been given a revelation of the resurrected Jesus for a purpose, he lived out his life as one accountable to that purpose and to the one who had given it to him—Jesus Christ.

Paul's Accountability to the Material He Taught

It has been stated earlier that the purposes of Paul's teaching ministry were to make the gospel known and to call for the response of faith from those who heard it. If those purposes were as simple as they might seem, there would have been no need for Paul to be a teacher. He could have carried out his mission by speaking in synagogues or on street corners wherever he had opportunity and then waiting for someone to say: "I believe." But it wasn't that simple. Paul wasn't content to just say the words. He struggled to put the words together in ways that they could be understood. He worked at explaining how the gospel touched every aspect of the believer's life. When he called for the response of faith, he had a clear notion about what that response was to. He referred to it in Galatians as "my gospel."

All of this meant that Paul knew himself to be accountable to the material he taught. He was faced with the challenge not only of making it known, but of clarifying it as well. Again, this is characteristic of teachers. Being accountable, they can't be satisfied with disseminating information—whether it be in lectures, programmed texts, or video cassettes. Their concern needs to be for learning as well as teaching; therefore they have to take into account the difficulties involved in learning. This Paul did. Those difficulties included, from his perspective, the very nature of the learner that turned away from the wisdom of God to follow its own delights and desires (Rom. 1:18ff.). Spiritual wisdom, Paul confessed, was a gift of the Spirit—a gift that was beyond his power to control. That did not mean, however, that he thought he was absolved from any accountability for clarifying the gospel for those he taught. There were at least three reasons why that need for clarification was so urgent for him, and therefore why it was so important for him to be a teacher. Those reasons are: the complex nature of the gospel; the enemies of Paul who attempted to distort the gospel as Paul taught it; and those who claimed to receive the gospel but did not understand its claim on their lives. Once these reasons have been explored, some suggestions will be offered as to how Paul demonstrated his accountability through the means he used to clarify the gospel for those he taught.

The complex and encompassing nature of the gospel.   When Paul preached and taught he literally brought good news. The message was good, and it was news. Most to whom he spoke had never heard anything like it before. After 2000 years of hearing the gospel, that fact can sometimes be overlooked. For those nurtured in a Christian environment, the gospel may seem deceptively simple. Paul seldom had the luxury of teaching in such a context. When he left the synagogues of the Jews, he found himself speaking to people who probably had little familiarity with the concepts and vocabulary, let alone the specifics of the faith story, that serve as the background for the gospel. Imagine the questions the Gentiles could have asked when they were first taught the concepts in Romans 5:

1. Justified? What does that mean, and who needs it? Why?
2. What is faith? Faith in what, or in whom? Where does faith come from?
3. Peace? Have I not been at peace with God? Is peace possible? How can Jesus give me peace?
4. God? Which of the gods is God?
5. Who was/is Jesus? Where did he come from? What did he do? What did he teach? What does "Christ" mean?
6. Lord? Do I need a Lord? Why is Jesus Lord, and what does that mean for my life?

These questions, and many more, must have occurred to those who first heard Paul teach. Many were like children who had never heard of God's love. The story of the Exodus and the words of the prophets were unknown. There were so many things these first students of Paul needed to know if they were to have some understanding of God's revelation in Jesus Christ. Once in the faith community, there was so much these new believers *wanted* to know. They wondered about the resurrection, the return of Jesus, and whether they could eat food offered first to idols. They wanted help in understanding their relationships to the state, to unbelievers, and to those who left the church. And, not least, there were organizational questions: Who had authority? What was the relationship of the parts to the whole?

Some, of course, thought they knew the answers to the questions. Others didn't always agree. Disputes arose, and sometimes there was bitterness. If it hadn't been recognized previously, it was soon discovered that the sweet simplicity of the gospel could become very complex before it became simple again. It brought its light to every area of life. "Paul, can you help us?" must have been a constant plea. "Tell us about Jesus and what it means to be a follower of the Way." So Paul taught them, again and again. If Paul had grown weary of the need for clarification, or given up hope for learning, he wouldn't have lasted as a teacher. But he didn't give up. Actually, it seems as though he looked forward to questions and saw them as opportunities to teach. He wrote to the Thessalonians:

> For what thanksgiving can we render to God for you for all the joy which we feel for your sake before our God, praying earnestly night and day that we may see you face to face and supply what is lacking in your faith? (1 Thess. 3:9-10).

Indeed throughout his ministry he followed his advice to the Galatians:

> And let us not grow weary in well-doing, for in due season we shall reap, if we do not lose heart. So then, as we have opportunity, let us do good to all men, and especially to those who are of the household of faith (Gal. 6:9-10).

What greater good could there have been for Paul than the stating, enlarging, and clarifying of the gospel that was the essence of his life?

Paul's attempts to clarify the gospel to those who opposed him.   If the complexity of the gospel was not enough, Paul had opponents who forced him to explain the difficulties they found in his teaching. For example, the Jews wanted to see signs that proved Jesus was the Messiah and Paul was his apostle. They had great expectations for the anointed one—he was to bring peace and restore the kingdom to Israel. What did Paul offer? A teacher, a crucifixion, and a claim of resurrection. Israel was still in bondage, therefore many Jews would not believe that the Messiah had come. Others had problems with Paul's teaching about the law. Did

Jesus replace the law, fulfill the law, make the law of no effect, or stand beside the law? Many were convinced that Paul had too little respect for the law. The Jews had cherished it as God's finest gift. It gave their life and nation definition. Now Paul was saying that the law was not the way of salvation. Who was he to make such a claim? Why, he even denied the importance of circumcision, the ancient sign of the covenant. Among the Jews who followed Jesus there were complaints about that.

There were other complaints against Paul as well. Wasn't he, really, throwing away the traditions of the fathers? Had he forgotten that the Jews were God's own chosen people? Wasn't he being a bit generous with the Gentiles? What did he mean by the phrase "justified by faith?" Didn't a person have to do something to be saved? "Come on, Paul. There's no way you can clarify those issues so that we can accept them," these opponents seemed to argue. Yet Paul kept trying to do just that.

Gentiles, too, challenged Paul. They wanted to know how it could be that the God of all creation could be the God of weak and backward Israel. How could a suffering man, dying on a cross, be more powerful than legions of soldiers, or the empire they defended? Where was the wisdom in weakness when strength was the wisdom of the day? "What have you to say to that, Paul?" they might have asked, and then added: "Yes, Paul, explain again all this business about your strength, explain it from your Roman prison."

What Paul had to say was the gospel. He continued to preach Christ crucified knowing that it was a stumbling block to the Jews and folly to the Gentiles (1 Cor. 1:23). He knew that he couldn't create faith in the gospel. That was the work of the Holy Spirit. In his teaching, however, he never gave up hope for clarifying for both Jews and Gentiles the thorny issues raised by the gospel. His letters, written expressions of his efforts, stand as records of his hopes. In his or any context, could one ask for anything more?

*Paul's attempts to clarify the gospel for those determined to misunder-
stand what he taught.*   There was a third category of people that
challenged Paul's efforts for clarity. He alluded to these people
in Romans 6, where he wrote: "What shall we say then? Are we
to continue to sin that grace might abound?" (v. 1). The question
suggests the problem. Paul taught that the law could not save,
no matter how hard a person tried to live by it. Salvation was a
gift that came through the grace of God. Grace was God's answer
to sin. Wherever sin abounded, grace abounded all the more.

As some heard St. Paul, at least to that point, what he taught
seemed almost too good to be true. They understood him to say
that they could do as they pleased—it didn't really matter how
they lived. Somehow these people were able to draw the conclusion
that sin was not only all right, it could actually be a definite
good. The more they sinned, they argued, the more grace they
could receive. What could be better than that: to live in this
world fulfilling one's passions and at the same time be confident
of God's heaven too?

Of all those who tested Paul's ability to be clear in his teaching,
these must have been the toughest. They listened to hear what
they wanted to hear and then closed their ears to more. What
they heard was only half the truth. They didn't, couldn't, or
wouldn't hear that God's grace, when it is received in faith, not
only forgives the sinner but transforms the sinner as well. Paul
tried to explain:

> Do you not know that all of us who have been baptized into
> Christ Jesus were baptized into his death? We were buried therefore
> with him by baptism into death, so that as Christ was raised from
> the dead by the glory of the Father, we too might walk in newness
> of life (Rom. 6:3-4).

And again:

> I appeal to you therefore, brethren, by the mercies of God, to
> present your bodies as a living sacrifice, holy and acceptable to

God, which is your spiritual worship. Do not be conformed to this world but be transformed by the renewal of your mind, that you may prove what is the will of God, what is good and acceptable and perfect (Rom. 12:1-2).

Whether or not these people ever understood the fullness of what Paul was teaching, one can almost be thankful for their challenge. In his attempts to counter their misconceptions, Paul was forced to clarify for himself and the early church the relationship between faith and life. It's a sign of life in the church that the struggle for a definition of piety confronts each new generation. Paul's letters continue to be a base from which to begin the discussion that leads to clarification.

Paul's Methods for Clarification

Paul went to great lengths in his attempts to clarify what he taught. Most teachers, however, aren't satisfied with the fact that they have tried to be clear. They look for evidence in their students that says: "I've got it. I understand what you are saying." But that's not the way it is, at least not all the time. Occasionally a teacher can complete a magnificent explanation to a student's question, yet the look on the student's face is one of greater confusion than when the teacher began. At that point the wheels begin to turn in the teacher's head: What can I do, what can I say, that will help her to understand? Paul must have seen more than his share of those looks, and he responded to them in a variety of ways.

Paul drew upon the resources of Scripture and the apostolic tradition. In Paul's time there was no New Testament. He drew from the Hebrew Scriptures quotations, references, and examples to clarify his teaching. At Thessalonica he ". . . argued . . . from the scriptures, explaining and proving that it was necessary for the Christ to suffer and to rise from the dead. . ." (Acts 17:2-3). Paul's sermons took the same approach. He began preaching to the people at Antioch of Pisidia by recounting, though quickly, much of the history of Israel to prepare his audience for the introduction of Jesus as the Christ. Then he concluded the sermon with several scriptural references about the resurrection and unbelief (Acts 13:13ff.).

Paul's letter to the Romans, his most instructional book, is filled with scriptural references. In at least half of the chapters Paul used quotations from the Old Testament. Throughout the letter there are references to Adam, Sarah, Hagar, Isaac, Jacob, Esau, and Moses. Out of a scriptural background he discussed the issues of circumcision, law, covenant, and promise—and presented Jesus as the fulfillment of God's love. To a tradition-minded people, Paul wanted to make clear that the gospel was rooted in the same soil as Judaism.

The apostolic tradition that was taking shape during his lifetime was also a resource for Paul. Two questions of the Corinthians are illustrative: one concerning the Lord's Supper and the other the resurrection. With respect to the former, the Corinthians were well on their way to making the sacrament a cause for division. Some people were bringing enough food to the agape feast to gorge themselves, while others had very little to eat. They were in danger of losing the unifying spirit of the meal. Paul would have none of that. Beginning with harsh criticism, he went on to clarify the tradition that continues to characterize the church's celebration of the Lord's Supper today (1 Cor. 11:17-34).

Among their many problems, the people in Corinth had to deal with doubts about the resurrection. Paul responded to the Corinthians by appealing to the teachings of the apostles. He wrote:

Now I would remind you, brethren, in what terms I preached to you the gospel, which you received, in which you stand, by which you are saved, if you hold it fast—unless you believed in vain.

For I delivered to you as of first importance what I also received, that Christ died for our sins in accordance with the scriptures, that he was buried, that he was raised on the third day in accordance with the scriptures, and that he appeared to Cephas, then to the twelve (1 Cor. 15:1-5).

Paul clarified his teaching through the use of illustrations.   The people in Corinth had difficulty in understanding the nature of the church that was taking shape among them. They were concerned about who should do what and who was in control. Paul attempted to clarify these organizational problems by appealing to the example of the human body and how it functioned. He wrote:

> For just as the body is one and has many members, and all the members of the body, though many, are one body, so it is with Christ. For by one Spirit we were all baptized into one body— Jews or Greeks, slaves or free—and all were made to drink of one Spirit (1 Cor. 12:12-13).

Paul went on to say that all the parts of the body have their own particular functions. Each and all of these functions are important to the well-being of the whole. Since the functions are all important, the organs that do them are equally important. If that's true of the human body, he argued, it's equally true of the church. Paul used the same illustration in his letter to the Romans (Rom. 12:3ff.).

Paul referred to his own faith and life as a means of clarification.   To those in Corinth who questioned the resurrection, Paul responded with words to this effect: "Why do you think I take the risks that I do? Do you think I'm stupid? If there weren't any resurrection, don't you suppose I would live for today and forget about tomorrow? Ah, but because there is a resurrection, I live and strive to do God's will." And what had that striving meant for Paul? Consider that question in the light of the following:

> Five times I have received at the hands of the Jews the forty lashes less one. Three times I have been beaten with rods; once I was stoned. Three times I have been shipwrecked; a night and a day I have been adrift at sea; on frequent journeys, in danger from rivers, danger from robbers, danger from my own people, danger from Gentiles, danger in the city, danger in the wilderness, danger at sea, danger from false brethren; in toil and hardship, through many a sleepless night, in hunger and thirst, often without food, in cold and exposure (2 Cor. 11:24-27).

Why did Paul do it? Of course, there was the hope of the resurrection. At the start of it, however, was the experience on the Damascus road. That event, to which Paul referred often, clarified many things. To the Galatians it demonstrated that Paul's apostleship was authentic—given directly by Christ (Gal. 1:11-12). To the Galatians, King Agrippa, Festus, and many more, it explained the tremendous change that marked Paul's life. Prior to it Paul had been a zealous defender of the law. "But," he wrote, "when he who had set me apart before I was born, and had called me through his grace, was pleased to reveal his Son to me, in order that I might preach him among the Gentiles. . .," his life was changed. From then on he preached and taught the gospel he had tried to destroy (Gal. 1:15ff.; Acts 26:1-23).

Whatever his previous convictions had been, whatever his previous values and dreams had focused upon, all had been set aside after the Damascus road experience. Reflecting back on his life, he wrote to the Philippians:

> But whatever gain I had, I counted as loss for the sake of Christ. Indeed, I count everything as loss because of the surpassing worth

of knowing Christ Jesus my Lord. For his sake I have suffered the loss of all things, and count them as refuse, in order that I may gain Christ and be found in him, not having a righteousness of my own, based on law, but that which is through faith in Christ, the righteousness from God that depends on faith; that I may know him and the power of his resurrection, and may share his sufferings, becoming like him in his death, that if possible I may attain the resurrection from the dead (Phil. 3:7-11).

Paul trusted the gracious God who had revealed himself in Jesus Christ and who through that revelation had transformed Paul's life. It was this faith, and the consequent transformation in life, that Paul yearned to see in those he taught. As an example he set out before them his experience, his faith, and his life. He couldn't give, or arrange for, the same experiences for others. He did, however, seek to clarify both faith and life by pointing to his own.

Paul used reminders as a means of clarification.   One of the expectations of education, especially in the authority model, is that students will remember what they have been taught. Without remembering the content, a significant part of the purpose of education is lost. Most teachers using this model are aware, however, of the likelihood that students will forget. A primary concern, then, is to find means that assist learners to remember.

While remembering has value for itself, it is even more important as a basis for thinking on the higher levels of the cognitive scale as described by Benjamin Bloom. Memory is the most elementary level on this scale, yet at the same time it is essential to all other levels of thinking. Information, Bloom pointed out, allowed one to do analysis, synthesis, and evaluation.

Paul didn't know anything about the forgetting curves that learning theorists today have charted, but he did know that people forget. He also knew that when people could not remember the basics of the faith, it would not be possible for them to grow in their understanding of the gospel. Realizing this, Paul's teaching kept returning to the center of the faith. He was convinced that if people forgot "Jesus Christ and him crucified," nothing else they remembered really mattered.

Of all his letters, Galatians seems to be the best example of Paul's concern to remind his learners of the essentials of the faith. The congregation in Galatia either had lost, or was in danger of losing, all clarity regarding the center of the faith. Paul's letter is a series of reminders: his authority as an apostle, his equality with the disciples, the emptiness of the law and the power of the gospel, and the covenant of promise. Paul wrote the letter in a mood something like that of a teacher who has just finished reading some very poor final examination papers. He couldn't understand if these people had forgotten, had misunderstood what he had taught, or had allowed themselves to be misled. No wonder he wrote: "I am perplexed about you" (Gal. 4:20). He was not so discouraged, however, that he gave up on the congregation. His letter was intended to remind and to clarify the gospel he had taught them.

The Corinthians, too, had their problems with remembering what they had been taught. Being concerned about this, and unable to go to Corinth himself, Paul sent his representative to keep fresh the memory of the gospel he taught. He alluded to that in the following:

> I do not write this to make you ashamed, but to admonish you as my beloved children. For though you have countless guides in Christ, you do not have many fathers. For I became your father in Christ Jesus through the gospel. I urge you, then, be imitators of me. Therefore I sent to you Timothy, my beloved and faithful child in the Lord, to remind you of my ways in Christ, as I teach them everywhere in every church. Some are arrogant, as though I were not coming to you. But I will come to you soon, if the Lord

wills, and I will find out not the talk of these arrogant people but their power (1 Cor. 4:14-19).

Again, Paul wrote in the tone of a schoolmaster. He was concerned for what these people seemed to have forgotten and for those who were teaching what they didn't understand. Both needed to be reminded of the basics of the gospel, and Paul was determined to meet that need.

If Paul's letters to them are any indication, the Thessalonians were especially interested in the second coming of Jesus. Like students who keep returning to the same questions, not satisfied with the responses they have been given, they wanted to know what it would be like when Jesus came. Picking up on their questions, Paul could not resist writing: "Do you not remember that when I was still with you I told you this?" (2 Thess. 2:5). Then he went on to explain again what he had taught them. He was willing to remind them.

On at least one occasion Paul seems to have written as much to satisfy his own desire to be clear as to try to clarify the thinking of his readers. He began his letter to the Romans with the acknowledgment that their faith was ". . . proclaimed in all the world" (Rom. 1:8). Though it was the courteous thing to say to this congregation located at the heart of the empire, there must have been truth in what he wrote. He concluded the letter in a similar vein:

> I myself am satisfied about you, my brethren, that you yourselves are full of goodness, filled with all knowledge, and able to instruct one another. But on some points I have written to you very boldly by way of reminder, because of the grace given me by God . . . (Rom. 15:14ff.).

All of Paul's letters, with the exception of Romans, were written reminders of what Paul had taught in person. He knew these reminders were necessary because people did forget and, having forgotten, they could get confused about both the gospel and its implications. In his letters Paul clarified the foundations upon which the church was built. Through the centuries his letters have continued to serve the same function. As Anders Nygren pointed out, it is in being reminded of the basics written in Romans that the church has found the resources for reformation.

Present-day educators would argue that accountability on the part of the teacher for presenting material in ways that can be understood is still only part of the picture. The further question is: Did the students learn? That issue can be raised with respect to Paul as well. As a result of all of his efforts and his deep sense of commitment to the gospel, did those who heard Paul understand the gospel he preached and taught, and was their reponse faithful to it? One could raise even one more question: How clear was Paul in his own understanding of what he taught? Well, Paul admitted he didn't know as much as he would have liked to know. To the Corinthians he wrote: "For our knowledge is imperfect. . . . For now we see in a mirror dimly, but then face to face. Now I know in part, then I shall understand fully, even as I have been fully understood" (1 Cor. 13:9ff.).

Not knowing everything, not being able to answer every question completely, didn't keep Paul from teaching. If he didn't know all the details, he was sure of the themes that he taught and was willing to be accountable for them. He had no doubts about his apostleship, and he staked his life on it (Gal. 1:11—2:21). He was confident of the love and mercy of God and lived as one totally dependent upon God's grace (Rom. 5:6-11; 8:31-39). He was sure that the just shall live by faith, and he defended his conviction against all who questioned or denied it (Rom. 5:1-5; Gal. 2:16ff.; Eph. 2:8-9). He was convinced that God was at work in the preaching and teaching of the gospel, and he spent his life doing both (Rom. 1:13-17; 10:14-15). There is an unmistakable congruity in Paul's thoughts and actions, a congruity that is evidence of a profound self-understanding and an account-ability to his own identity.

As for his being understood by others, the evidence certainly suggests that he was. Two groups noted earlier, the believers and the ones who opposed Paul, are both witnesses. By all their questions the former acknowledged their awareness of the tremendous implications of what Paul taught. They realized that if what Paul taught was true, then their entire lives would have to be affected by it. By giving them a vision of the majesty, power, and love of God, they had been launched on a pilgrimage of searching and growing, a journey they made with their teacher, Paul.

The opposition understood Paul well enough to know that they were threatened by what he taught. In fact, the extent of the opposition may be one of the surest signs of Paul's effectiveness as a teacher. He wasn't vague. He didn't leave people wondering where he stood. Clearly Paul invited the opposition to abandon the seemingly comfortable ground of the law and exchange it for trust in the grace of God. He asked them to surrender their claims to righteousness and accept the righteousness of God. It was an awesome thing Paul asked of them. They understood that, even if they did not grasp what lay beyond. With them Paul argued, wept, and pleaded. He prayed that they be given the faith that leads to understanding. In all his struggles with the opposition he never forgot that at one time he had been one of them, a violent enemy of the gospel.

Even the mischievous ones who deliberately distorted the gospel to meet their own ends were something of an asset to Paul. He was aware of them and the ruinous effects they could have upon the church. They provided an example of how the gospel could be twisted by people who listened to only half of the story. In his response to them. Paul may not have convinced these oppor-tunists of their misunderstandings, but he did give the faithful new insights and clarity about the relationship between faith and life.

I doubt if Paul ever assigned papers for his students to write or asked them to take tests that demonstrated what they had learned. Nevertheless, he certainly had his expectations. He expressed them throughout his letters and, presumably, in his day-to-day preaching and teaching. What he taught has stood the test of time; as the architects of St. Paul's Cathedral illustrated, he became a great teacher of the church. That greatness arose in no small measure because he was consistently and constantly accountable to the gospel—to the material that he taught.

Paul's Accountability to Those He Taught

It is assumed that a teacher's accountability extends in some measure to student learning. Paul's included that, but extended far beyond it as well. First, he believed that what he taught could never be discovered by learners working on their own. Someone had to reveal it to them. Second, he believed that the understanding of those he taught had been darkened by sin. They themselves were sinners, living outside the righteousness of God. Third, those he taught were also the beloved—the ones for whom Christ had died. Those Paul taught were not just learners, as important a realization as that is. They were persons of value. As he wrote to the Corinthians, they had been purchased at great cost to God. They needed to know that and to be informed about what that meant for their lives (1 Cor. 6:20). They needed to know that in order that they, too, could be accountable. Fourth, these were the persons who were the church—the church entrusted with the ministry of the gospel to all the world. The response of faith that Paul called for included enlistment in the service of the cross. To serve, the people of God needed to learn and be enabled for ministry.

That service, Paul believed, would eventually bring the world to the foot of the cross. It was an astounding vision for a church that must have seemed small and inadequate when measured against the powers and institutions that stood over against it. Indeed, it was only his confidence in the power of Christ, the head of the church, that could have allowed it. Yet, in the careful work of teaching, Paul labored to enable the church to withstand the first waves of persecution that would soon break in upon it and to provide direction and content for the great missionary enterprise that would bring the gospel to all the earth. Paul's sense of accountability, working faithfully with those he had been given to teach, still provides a sound base for the work of the church today—that of carefully teaching the few in order that they be enabled to reach the many. That's the servant role to which Paul believed he had been called.

Having come that far, it can be seen that Paul's sense of accountability made a full circle. It began in his call by God to be an apostle. It ran through his concern for clarity in the teaching and learning of the gospel. It continued in his deep commitment to those he taught. Finally, it came again to the one who had called him, before he was born, to be a servant. To him, first, last, and always, Paul desired to be accountable—not as one under the law, but under Christ, the one who had redeemed him and made him his own.

For Reflection

1. What part, if any, does accountability play in the teaching ministry of the church today?

2. If you are a teacher, to whom or to what do you have a sense of accountability?

3. In what ways do you see teachers in the church being held accountable for their teaching?

4. Is accountability in the church today viewed differently than the ideas and practices of Paul as presented in this chapter?

5. What would you do if you thought there was someone in the church school who was teaching something contrary to the gospel? What do you think Paul would have done? Is this a concern for accountability?

CHAPTER FIVE ══════════════

THE WAYS
WE
LEARN

It would be hard to imagine any certified teacher today not knowing the names and work of Jean Piaget and B. F. Skinner. These people and so many more have done research in an attempt to discover how learning occurs. Yet, in spite of all the time and effort expended in this search, social scientiests continue to disagree on the issue.

As one peruses the literature on learning theory written in the last several decades, one could be overwhelmed. A question presents itself: Without the benefit of all this data, how did teachers of previous generations do their work, and how did anyone learn from teachers who hadn't the benefit of all this information to guide them in their teaching? The question seems to imply some doubts about the value of all this research. That is not my intent. Rather, I would prefer to argue that earlier teachers did have some notions about how people learn and that, no matter how poorly they were taught, there were some who, in past generations, learned a great deal.

Occasionally one reads a comment by a current writer that is rather disdainful of teachers like Paul, not least with respect to their lack of sophistication about learning. To be sure, Paul was not research-oriented. The scientific method was unknown to him. It's probably also true that Paul didn't spend a lot of time reflecting on either the methods or questions of learning theorists. Nevertheless, both explicitly and implicitly, we can find in his writings some keen insights about learning. It's evident that Paul allowed for a variety of ways of learning, and in that he probably shared the outlook of most teachers, even today. Those ways included revelation, experience, reason, imitation, and reinforcement.

Learning and Teaching through Revelation

By revelation I mean coming to know something one could never know without having been told it in some fashion by another. For example, other people cannot know my thoughts unless I choose to make them known. They might guess, but I would have to verify whether or not they were correct before it could be said that they knew. In a very simple way, this is revelation.

Revelation was at the very heart of Paul's teaching. He believed that God's love, and his intent for creation, could not have been known except God had chosen to reveal it. Whether through inquiry, problem solving, self-examination, or reason—people could never have discovered the nature and extent of God's love on their own. Even if they had guessed it, they could not have been sure it was true without God confirming it in some way. For Paul this was a mystery, a secret hidden for generations, that God had to reveal if humankind was ever to know of it (Rom. 16:25ff.; 1 Cor. 2:7). A significant part of that hiddenness is the result of humankind's inability to see and understand the truth set before it in creation. Confronted with the reality of creation, humankind chose not to honor God as creator, and therefore God's glory had been exchanged for another. In so doing, humankind's understanding and vision had been darkened (Rom. 1:18-32; 3:9ff.).

Therefore, Paul argued, it was necessary for God to take the initiative in revealing himself. God began in the call to Abraham and the covenant he established with him. This covenant was sealed by faith (Rom. 4:16ff.). Through the centuries God continued to reveal his will to and through the children of Abraham. Finally, ". . . when the time had fully come, God sent forth his Son, born of woman, born under the law, to redeem those who were under the law, so that we might receive adoption as sons" (Gal. 4:4-5).

Paul shared the conviction of the fourth evangelist: "No one had ever seen God; the only Son, who is in the bosom of the Father, he has made him known" (John 1:18). In his letter to the Colossians Paul put it this way:

> He [Jesus] is the image of the invisible God, the first-born of all creation; for in him all things were created, in heaven and on earth, visible and invisible, whether thrones or dominions or principalities or authorities—all things were created through him and for him. He is before all things, and in him all things hold together. He is the head of the body, the church; he is the beginning, the first-born from the dead, that in everything he might be preeminent. For in him all the fullness of God was pleased to dwell, and through him to reconcile to himself all things, whether on earth or in heaven, making peace by the blood of his cross (Col. 1:15-20).

The apostle did not discover this on his own. It came to him as a growing realization that began on the Damascus road. Prior to that day he had understood Christians to be his enemies. He had been zealous beyond all others to protect the traditions of Israel as he then understood them. Then Jesus revealed himself to Paul. By revelation he learned what he could not have learned in any other way—that the one he was persecuting was the Son of God (Acts 9:1ff.).

Once Jesus had made himself known to him, Paul returned to the Scriptures that he already accepted as God's revelation. Now, however, he read them in a different light. The Law and the Prophets became for him signs that pointed to Jesus and his cross and resurrection. The revelation Paul received became the cornerstone of his teaching. He wrote to the Romans: ". . . I will not venture to speak of anything except what Christ has wrought through me to win obedience from the Gentiles, by word and deed . . ." (Rom. 15:18).

Paul's definition of a teacher as an authority-enabler, with the emphasis upon authority, was largely determined by the influence of revelation as a way to learn. An indirect approach may be helpful in learning many things, but Paul was convinced that it would never lead to the discovery of the gospel. Quite the contrary, to the wisdom of the age mercy seemed less reasonable than justice, love weaker than chariots and spears, a cross an unseemly throne, and resurrection an unlikely hope. Yet that which seemed so contrary to the wisdom of the age was the very essence of the revelation God had given in his Son, Jesus. This was what Paul had received. On the basis of the authority of the one who had given it, Paul could do no other than preach and teach it (1 Cor. 1:10—2:13).

Paul had no illusions about the difficulties involved in teaching and learning through revelation. The same barriers that had darkened the human mind before the coming of Jesus still had to be overcome. The same pride that had asserted itself as the measure of all things still rebelled at the notion of submission and obedience to any lord—even the creating and redeeming Lord, Jesus Christ. But Paul believed that beyond all his efforts was the authority and power of the Holy Spirit. His greatest concern, trust in the gospel, was finally the Spirit's work, not his. All he could do, which was a great deal, was be a faithful witness in representing the revelation given to him (1 Cor. 4:1-2).

Learning through Experience

It's common knowledge that learning comes with experience. Somewhat less commonly acknowledged is the realization that some of the most profound of all human qualities are learned by experience. Among these are trust, peace, joy, and contentment. These qualities are intrinsic to the life that is lived in relationship with God. Trust is the key. It is the ability to give oneself over into the hands of another, sure that the other will be constant in presence, love, and support. In that surety there is peace, joy, and contentment.

Still less common, perhaps, is the awareness that Paul recognized the connection between the learning of trust and experience. He alluded to it in his letter to the Philippians:

> Not that I complain of want; for I have learned, in whatever state I am, to be content. I know how to be abased; and I know how to abound; in any and all circumstances I have learned the secret of facing plenty and hunger, abundance and want. I can do all things in him who strengthens me (Phil. 4:11-13).

This text provides a springboard into a discussion on learning by experience. To begin, Paul points out that he wasn't born content. He had to learn it. Further, contentment was not simply a matter of feeling all right about himself, being comfortable in any situation. Nor was it something that he could achieve once and for all. This was something Paul had to work through many times in his life. What he had learned was how to do that—by placing himself in the care of God. He had learned to trust God with his life.

As in every aspect of his life following his conversion, this learning began in his relationship with Jesus. The love of God in Jesus was the bond that made trust possible. This assurance was given eloquent expression in his letter to the Romans:

> Who shall separate us from the love of Christ? Shall tribulation, or distress, or persecution, or famine, or nakedness, or peril, or sword? . . . No, in all these things we are more than conquerors through him who loved us. For I am sure that neither death, nor life, nor angels, nor principalities, nor things present, nor things to come, nor powers, nor height, nor depth, nor anything else in all creation, will be able to separate us from the love of God in Christ Jesus our Lord (Rom. 8:35ff.).

Paul's assurance that he could trust in the love of God began before he met Jesus on the Damascus road. From that moment, however, he learned it in dimensions previously unknown to him. Among his lessons were those of weakness, surrender, dependence, waiting, suffering, grief, separation, joy, and thanksgiving. In his life as an apostle to the Gentiles he experienced all of these and in them learned to trust Christ for all in this life and eternity.

In Philippians Paul marked the boundaries of his learning with the experience of plenty on the one hand and want on the other. Let us examine the evidence of the former. Paul had much to celebrate in his life. Wherever he went he had the satisfaction of seeing at least the beginnings of congregations that confessed faith in the gospel. Many of his letters conclude with greetings to a number of people who were close friends. These people loved, welcomed, and encouraged him in his work. They tried to protect him, without success, from the events that eventually developed in Jerusalem and led to his imprisonment.

There are many scales on which to measure plenty or, as it might be called today, success. On many of them Paul would have to be judged successful. The trouble with the scales is that most of them are so open-ended they seldom lead to contentment and trust. The old trap of "the more you have, the more you want" can be as inviting to the religious as to any other. Paul's ministry could have been for him a source of great discontent and mistrust. Being right about so many things, he could have insisted that he knew everything. There must have been times when he could have set himself up as the leader of a sect rather than a follower of Jesus. At the same time, a few converts could have made him anxious for more, a little growth cause for despair because there weren't as many responding to the gospel as he might have hoped. Like others, having worked so hard in the expectation that the Christ would come again soon, Paul could have tired of waiting for his appearance.

Paul learned that having plenty didn't guarantee control. He learned that believing in the return of Jesus in power didn't make it happen according to his plan and efforts. As often as not, being a servant of God meant waiting—waiting for God to act. It's hard work, this waiting, and it both depends on and leads to trust. From the Old Testament Paul had learned something about trusting God. As he participated in the planting and growing of the church, and as he waited, he experienced God's grace and learned to trust even more. In this trust he found contentment.

Learning to trust God at the boundary of plenty is one thing. Experiencing it at the limit of personal suffering and want is quite another. Plenty tempts one to trust in self and become impatient with God. Want can lead to despair and unbelief. It is this latter boundary that seems to have provided the larger context for Paul's life. He acknowledged at least the possibility, if not the reality, of despair to the Corinthians (2 Cor. 4:7-12). Having admitted the possibility, he hurried on to say that his experience actually led to a more profound understanding of what it meant to trust God:

> For we do not want you to be ignorant, brethren, of the affliction we experienced in Asia; for we were so utterly, unbearably crushed

that we despaired of life itself. Why, we felt that we had received
the sentence of death; but that was to make us rely not on ourselves
but on God who raises the dead; he delivered us from so deadly a
peril, and he will deliver us; on him we have set our hope that he
will deliver us again (2 Cor. 1:8-10).

In Romans Paul stated the content of the gospel in such a way
that it would be difficult to separate it from the experience of
suffering. He wrote:

> Therefore, since we are justified by faith, we have peace with
> God through our Lord Jesus Christ. Through him we have obtained
> access to this grace in which we stand, and we rejoice in our hope
> of sharing the glory of God. More than that, we rejoice in our
> sufferings, knowing that suffering produces endurance, and en-
> durance produces character, and character produces hope, and hope
> does not disappoint us, because God's love has been poured into
> our hearts through the Holy Spirit which has been given to us
> (Rom. 5:1-5).

Suffering was the experience of the early church. Through the
example of the suffering Christ, Paul interpreted that universal
experience. Through it, he claimed, one learned to trust God.
That knowledge protected against the most dangerous of misconceptions—that of independence. In infancy and old age de-
pendency is not too hard to recognize. Between the two a myth
can be entertained, the myth of one's own power and immortality.
Suffering destroys the myth. It allows one to learn the qualities
that are needed once the notion of independence has been shat-
tered, the qualities of endurance, character, and hope.

Paul was not only aware that experience teaches, but that what
it teaches can be unpredictable. Plenty doesn't necessarily lead to
gratitude, and suffering doesn't always result in trust. He apparently struggled with the problem himself and learned to live
with both. He knew that others needed help in understanding

both their experiences and Paul's. He assured the Philippians that his imprisonment in Rome was a blessing (Phil. 1:12ff.). He wrote to the Corinthians that his sufferings were having positive results in his life and that they were not more than he could bear (2 Cor. 1:8ff.; 4:7ff.).

With respect to the suffering of others, Paul wrote: "We know that in everything God works for good with those who love him, who are called according to his purpose" (Rom. 8:28). In the larger sense, he told the Corinthians that neither plenty nor want should be allowed to separate them from God, not because they were so strong, but because God was faithful (1 Cor. 10:12ff.).

Experience can be easily misinterpreted, especially when one is left alone to reflect. Despair and pride are the temptations of the solitary. For that reason Paul encouraged the church to share in the experiences of all of its people—to weep with those who wept and to rejoice with those who were happy (Rom. 12:15). For the same reason he constantly urged his congregations to interpret their lives in terms of the gospel. If experience led to the temptation of pride, Paul reminded them that Jesus, though he was God, humbled himself. If the temptation was despair, he recalled again that Jesus suffered and died and that in his resurrection the complete faithfulness of God was made known.

Paul knew that the boundaries of want and plenty had much to teach. He didn't seem much interested in pushing his people in the direction of one or the other. He must have assumed that life would have enough of both. He was also aware that experiences gained at either end of the spectrum would have considerable effect upon learning trust, peace, joy, and contentment. What was learned about these was dependent upon returning again and again to the revelation and upon having the mind of Christ (Phil. 2:1ff.).

Learning through Reason

Though he was convinced that it could neither create faith nor lead to the discovery of the gospel, reason did have a place in the learning theory of Paul. His own ability to think rationally and his expectation that others would do so are evident on nearly every page of his letters. Few single texts illustrate this better than 1 Corinthians 15.

At least some in Corinth, though accepting the resurrection of Jesus, doubted that they would be raised from the dead. Paul's response to this issue graphically illustrated his use of reason and his demand that others use reason as well. He began by stating that Jesus' resurrection was at the center of God's revelation and his own preaching. Paul went on to say that a denial of their own resurrection was a denial of that of Jesus, of his preaching, of the forgiveness of sins, and of hope. Having dealt with his opponents' major premise and its conclusions, Paul turned to his own:

> But in fact Christ has been raised from the dead, the first fruits of those who have fallen asleep. For as by a man came death, by a man has come also the resurrection of the dead. For as in Adam all die, so also in Christ shall all be made alive. But each in his own order: Christ the first fruits, then at his coming those who belong to Christ. Then comes the end, when he delivers the kingdom to God the Father after destroying every rule and every authority and power. For he must reign until he has put all his enemies under his feet. The last enemy to be destroyed is death (1 Cor. 15:20-26).

This is a powerful argument deriving from Paul's major premise: Jesus has been raised from the dead. Paul knew, however, that he wasn't done. He continued to reason with the Corinthians along other lines. Some wanted to know about the kind of body there would be in the resurrection. Paul responded on the basis of logic. The seed, he wrote, was not like the plant which grew from it, yet they are related. So the resurrected body will not be the same as the earthly body—it will be spiritual, not physical. God has chosen to create in the physical world an infinite variety of bodies. Isn't it reasonable to assume that God will choose the nature of the spiritual body as well?

In this passage from Corinthians Paul's argument then turned back to his major premise and the content of the gospel. God, he wrote, raised Jesus from the dead. Jesus gained the victory. God had given this victory to the Corinthians through Jesus Christ. There was no need for doubt or fear. As surely as Christ had been raised from the dead, so would they be raised up (1 Cor. 15:51ff.).

As Paul was developing his own line of thought, he asked his readers to do some thinking of their own. What, he asked them, did they think he was doing if there wasn't any resurrection? Why should he risk his life for a message that he wasn't sure about? Wasn't he as capable as anyone of concluding that one must enjoy today if there wasn't any tomorrow? But he did risk his life day after day. Couldn't they draw any conclusions from that? Then he told them in so many words: "Use your heads—think!" (1 Cor. 15:20-34).

The exhortation to think presumes at least two things: something to think about, and the ability to think. Both are concerns for the teacher in Paul's approach to teaching. Students are expected to reason about the content they have been given. The most important part of the content for Paul, of course, was the gospel: God's love revealed in the suffering, death, and resurrection of Jesus.

Though Paul seems to have assumed that his hearers could reason, he didn't take it for granted that they would, or that they would think as logically as they might. A part of his responsibility was to help them. He did this by pointing out errors where they existed and by providing examples of logical patterns of thought (1 Cor. 5:1ff.; 5:9ff.; 6:8ff.). His letters show little concern with helping others to learn *how* to think. It may be unfair to even suggest that they should. Letters are not educational texts—at least not usually. In his personal teaching Paul could have been very concerned with this, but there is no way of knowing. What is apparent is that Paul used deductive reasoning in developing his theology, and he expected others to be able to follow his line of thought. If it can't be said that he helped his students to learn *how* to think, he did encourage them to imitate him, including his ability to reason. This leads into the fourth way in which Paul thought learning occurred—imitation, or, to use the more positive term of today, modeling.

Learning through Imitation

Paul did not make the mistake of equating formal education with learning. He knew that people learned apart from those moments when teachers were purposefully involved in teaching them. He recognized that what was learned informally had a direct influence on what was learned through instruction. This awareness is illustrated in two ways in his letters. One is his emphasis upon experience which was discussed earlier. The other is the many references he made to learning by imitation. Let's examine these references in the context of the following questions.

Is imitation a sound way to learn?   Some, for a variety of reasons, would be inclined to say no. One reason is its apparent failure to take into account the uniqueness of the individual. If learners are expected to imitate others, their freedom to develop their own personhood seems to be inhibited. Another reason is the nature of the learning itself. Imitation seems to be a very elementary form of learning that cannot be compared in any favorable way with analysis or problem solving. Indeed, it could be argued that imitation works against creativity and scientific inquiry.

Whatever its shortcomings, however, there is no doubt that humans learn through imitation. It's the reason why children in

China speak Chinese and those in Sweden don't. It also explains why Americans of an Asiatic background eat rice and those from northern Europe eat potatoes. Language, eating habits, and other more subtle patterns of behavior are learned early in life—to a large extent through imitation.

Imitation points to the importance of the environment in learning. Few people are taught to smoke cigarettes. Those who do smoke learn how by watching others. High school students aren't necessarily taught in any formal sense how they are to dress and behave if they want to be accepted in a certain group. They learn by imitating the behavior of those in the group to which they want to belong. Once they have imitated the behavior, it isn't unlikely that they will begin to think like those they have imitated. What this means, of course, is that behavior can affect thinking just as thinking can change behavior.

Paul was very much aware of the importance of informal learning. In several of his letters he warned his people to stay away from those who distorted the gospel. These, he said, could not help but have a negative influence upon them (1 Cor. 15:33; 5:9ff.; Titus 1:10ff.). Interestingly, he did not encourage separation from the world. He also realized that his own behavior was being observed. He had had experience with those who had been quick to criticize either his teaching or his behavior or both, so he worked hard at making the one consistent with the other. Obviously his invitation to have others imitate him was extended only after careful consideration (1 Cor. 9:1ff.; 2 Thess. 3:8-9; 1 Thess. 2:9ff.).

There was also the complexity of the gospel to be taken into account. Paul knew that it wasn't all that self-evident. If people wanted and needed a clear picture of the gospel at work in a person's life, Paul was willing to have them look at him. Having seen that picture, as inadequate as it may have been, he encouraged them to do what he did. To the Philippians he wrote: "What you have learned and received and heard and seen in me, do; and the God of peace will be with you" (Phil. 4:9). Paul must have been convinced that by their doing the Philippians would come to better understand the gospel

What kind of a person would dare, would have the confidence, to offer himself as a model for others?   There's no doubt that Paul did (1 Cor. 4:15ff.; 11:1; Phil. 3:17; 1 Thess. 1:6; 2 Thess. 3:9). Many would not be so bold today. In fact, many teachers might resent having to serve as models for those they teach. Such a notion would have been foreign to Paul. He could not separate his person from what he taught. His life reflected what contemporary educators often set as a goal—integration. Paul's attitudes, goals, values, beliefs, and behavior were so closely identified with what he taught and wanted others to learn that it wasn't possible to differentiate the man from the teacher. It was the measure of this integration that allowed him to dare to invite others to imitate him.

But what was it about this integration that gave Paul such confidence? The key to that question is that Paul, himself, was following a model. He had no pretensions about his own greatness or how helpful it would be if others were simply like him, the man Paul. He didn't even claim to own himself (1 Cor. 6:19-20). In all things he subjected himself to Christ. The more his life could be like Christ's, the more content he would be.

Paul's submission to Christ was not a choice he made because he had no other alternatives. As he noted on several occasions, if he had wanted to boast, he could have (Phil. 3:41ff.; 2 Cor. 11:16ff.; Gal. 1:13ff.). Paul was a learned man, gifted in speech, with a promising future in Judaism. He moved in the circles of the wise and powerful with ease. All of this, said Paul, he was more than willing to give up in order to follow—to imitate—another (Phil. 3:7ff.).

Clearly if one is to submit one's own life to another, the choice of model is critical. Paul believed that his model was no less than

God's Son. Having given his life over to him, he encouraged others to do the same. What he hoped for was not so much that others would be imitators of Paul, but of Christ who lived in him—the Christ who had emptied himself and given himself for the salvation of all (Phil. 2:5ff.). Indeed, this is precisely what Jesus had taught his disciples (Mark 9:35ff.). In the obedience of the cross, Jesus revealed the love and faithfulness of God. Through his own obedience to Christ, Paul also discovered God's unfailing support. If others did the same, they too would make that discovery. Paul's confidence was in God. He firmly believed that in the imitation of Jesus, God's power and love would become known.

Another dimension to Paul's confidence is found in his call to apostleship. He was sure that God had set him apart for his ministry. He described himself as an ambassador for Christ (2 Cor. 5:20). As such his life was bound to the one he represented. If others could not make this connection between who he was and what he did, his office would have been a mockery. But by the grace of God he was what he was (1 Cor. 15:10). He had learned to live in submission to Christ, and in obedience he had discovered peace, joy, and contentment. With bold but very simple confidence he could say to King Agrippa ". . . I would to God that not only you but also all who hear me this day might become such as I am . . ." (Acts 26:29). If the life and thought of St. Paul is any indication, the value and possibilities for learning by imitation have been too much underrated, especially when it comes to endurance, character, hope, and trust.

Learning through Reinforcement

It's quite amazing that it took until the 20th century for the formal learning theory of reinforcement to take shape. It's equally surprising that while it has now been rather well-documented, it's still so often ignored. For example, parents continue to beat their children with such enthusiasm that child abuse has become a national scandal. Some trained teachers continue to resort to sarcasm as a primary means of classroom control. There must be times when B. F. Skinner gets discouraged with the amount of punishment and negative reinforcement in many homes and classrooms. When those times come, he might be encouraged by the letters of Paul.

Paul knew enough about motivation and positive reinforcement to prompt him to commend those thoughts and actions that he wanted repeated. In each of his letters he rewards something with words of praise. He remarked to the Romans and Thessalonians that news of their sound faith and activity had reached him (Rom. 1:8; 1 Thess. 1:6-10). After reading his letters, wouldn't these people be encouraged to continue in the same pattern? In a later letter to the Thessalonians he commended them for the way they were growing in their love for each other (2 Thess. 1:3ff.). Wouldn't it be correct to assume that they would conclude, after reading that, that they were on the right track in their understanding of the gospel and its implications for the way they lived together? In a similar way he wrote to the Colossians telling them how much he rejoiced in their good order and the firmness of their faith (Col. 2:5). Knowing the authority that Paul's name carried, the Philippians could not help but be pleased to know he considered them his partners in the gospel, pleased and also motivated to strive with him (Phil. 1:3ff.).

By no stretch of the imagination could Paul be called a behaviorist. He did, however, know the power of love and that the nature of love is to build up rather than tear down (1 Cor. 14:12; 1 Thess. 5:11). Wherever Paul saw evidence of this building, he reinforced it. And, as every behaviorist knows, those actions that are positively reinforced are going to be repeated—and learned. In its way, then, reinforcement contributed to the growth and the theological content of the Christian faith.

There are few surprises in Paul's approaches to learning. His views are consistent with how he had learned and the model of teaching he adopted for his own. There was little in his experience, or in that of the world at that time, that could have led him into scientific inquiry on the one hand, or to question the authority of revelation on the other. Revelation was integral to his Judaic heritage. Reason continued to occupy the throne upon which the Greek philosophers had placed it. Example, reinforcement, and experience, as ways of learning, are part of that common sense that is only too evident once it has been pointed out. It's a tribute to Paul's brilliance and openness that he could find a place for all these approaches in his model of teaching and learning.

For Reflection

1. Think for a moment about something significant you have learned about the Christian faith or about being a Christian. How did you learn it? Was it through revelation, experience, reason, reinforcement—or some combination of these?
2. In your opinion, what are the primary means the church uses in its educational ministry today to assist others to learn the gospel?
3. How do these means compare with those discussed in this chapter?
4. What are some ways by which the church could enrich its teaching ministry through more varied approaches to learning?
5. If you are a teacher, what could you do to stimulate learning in your classes through a variety of approaches to learning?
6. What do you see as the relationship between total life experiences and the formal instruction provided by the church?

CHAPTER SIX ══════════════

PAUL'S
TEACHING
STYLE

Teaching style refers to how teachers go about their work and how they relate to their students. Many factors influence what a particular teacher's style will be. Several of these have been noted in previous chapters: the teacher's definition of the teaching role, the teacher's understanding of the learner and how learning occurs, and the material the teacher is expected to teach. Other important dimensions to style are the personality of the teacher and the gifts she or he has for teaching. Each of these factors is capable of being expressed in a variety of ways, and teachers put them together in ways that are peculiar to them. Thus each teacher's style is one of his or her own making.

Describing a teacher's style is a difficult task. To do it justice one really needs to be with and experience the teacher. To understand and appreciate it, one should observe it in the spontaneous moment when the personality of the teacher, the content, the readiness of students, and the environment converge in that activity called teaching.

This being the case, the difficulties involved in describing

Paul's style are obvious. All that's available to us are the written records of Acts and his epistles. From them we can only infer those characteristics that seem to describe him and his teaching. The picture that emerges is left, finally, to the reader's imagination. Keeping that in mind, the following are characteristics of Paul's style that provide some substance for that emerging image.

Paul Was Knowledgeable

While a teacher's knowledge is something that is generally taken for granted, it's something that has to be particularly affirmed in the case of Paul. The reason is that some have understood him to be rather negative about the worth of knowledge. This interpretation of the apostle was probably a factor in the church's opposition to the scientific discoveries that came at the dawn of the enlightenment. Others appealed to Paul in defense of the argument that ignorance is a more sound base for faith than wisdom.

As much as anywhere, this interpretation comes out of Paul's letters to the Corinthians. The Greeks had a deep appreciation for wisdom. It was an integral part of their heritage. They apparently allowed these roots to create problems in their understanding of the gospel. Following are just a few of Paul's comments intended to counter this influence:

> Has not God made foolish the wisdom of the world? For since, in the wisdom of God, the world did not know God through wisdom, it pleased God through the folly of what we preach to save those who believe. . . .
>
> For consider your call, brethren; not many of you were wise according to worldly standards . . . but God chose what is foolish in the world to shame the wise. . . .
>
> When I came to you, brethren, I did not come proclaiming to you the testimony of God in lofty words or wisdom . . . that your faith might not rest in the wisdom of men but in the power of God. . . (1 Cor. 1:20—2:5).

Comments such as these, along with his warnings against the wisdom of false teachers (Col. 2:8), could lead one to the conclusion that Paul thought that knowledge was an enemy of faith. In one sense that was true—when human wisdom was allowed to stand in judgment over God's revelation in Christ. Apart from that, Paul himself was an intellectual who extended the frontiers of knowledge. Much in Acts and the epistles supports this view.

There is first Paul's extension of the gospel into all areas of human life and thought—into the world far beyond the boundaries of Palestine. As the gospel became increasingly inclusive, the challenge to confront other religions and patterns of thought also became greater. As the apostle to the Gentiles, Paul made an invaluable contribution in meeting that challenge. As needs were met in defining the faith, the content of the faith grew. Along with that growth came greater demands on teachers to be knowledgeable. Paul himself was a pattern for this well-informed person.

Paul was not above boasting when it served his purpose to do so. Among the things of which he could be proud was his learning, the second evidence of his being knowledgeable. He wrote to the Galatians that in his early years he had progressed in Judaism beyond most his same age (Gal. 1:14). In Acts Paul is more definite about his background. Born in Tarsus, he had grown up in Jerusalem and been a student of Gamaliel. As such, he was ". . . educated according to the strict manner of the law of our fathers" (Acts 22:3).

It was this kind of education that equipped him to lead the attack in persecuting the church before his conversion. After his conversion he turned his attention to the study of the Scriptures with an entirely new principle of interpretation. In them he now saw the promise of a crucified, risen, and redeeming Lord. Just as he had excelled in Judaism, he now threw himself into the study of the emerging Christian faith—and became its chief advocate in the Gentile world. In this enterprise Paul knew he was not intellectually inferior to those of his contemporaries who were also Christian teachers. He wrote to the Corinthians:

> I think that I am not in the least inferior to these superlative apostles. Even if I am unskilled in speaking, I am not in knowledge; in every way we have made this plain to you in all things (2 Cor. 11:5-6).

One wonders if his comments about his speaking ability weren't more for the sake of modesty than fact. They could possibly refer to his education in the Jewish tradition rather than the oratorical school of Quintilian that was highly valued at the time. In any case, Paul must have been a powerful and persuasive speaker—at least if the people in Lystra are to be believed (Acts 14:8ff.).

The attention Paul commanded from others is yet another evidence of his learning. Wherever he went he got something of a hearing. Philosophers paused to listen in Athens (Acts 17:19). Leaders of the synagogue in Rome were open to hear his opinions (Acts 28:22). In his defense before Festus and King Agrippa, the Roman governor detected an intellectual brilliance that he thought had gone mad. It was an opinion not shared by the Jewish king, who understood the background out of which Paul spoke (Acts 26:1-29). His ability to gain an audience with the learned illustrates that, with them, Paul was among his peers.

Finally, if there was nothing else, his letters alone would be sufficient to demonstrate Paul's learning and natural intellectual ability. One may argue with his conclusions, but there's no doubt that a sharp, logical mind was behind them. The one we meet in the letters may not be precisely the person Paul was in the flesh. He even admitted to that possibility when writing to one of his congregations (2 Cor. 10:7ff.). The writer and the person, however, could not have been significantly different persons. Paul was a teacher who knew his subject. He could draw from the Old Testament all he needed and then some, to illustrate his points. He had thought about the Scriptures and synthesized them into a coherent whole. If not a classical scholar, he was at home in Greek philosophy. In addition, his learning was not limited to what he could gain through formal education. Paul was an observer of human behavior and spent a good deal of time reflecting on what he saw. He had, himself, experienced a great deal. He had lived a life of trust and service and knew of what he spoke when he commended that life to others. When it came to the gospel and the resurrection of Christ, he preached and taught it as the most sure thing he could possibly have known.

Being confronted by Paul the teacher must have been quite an experience. When Paul listened, the speaker could almost be sure that Paul understood what was being said. When Paul spoke, it was out of a rich reservoir of knowledge and experience. This must have been one of the first things that people noted about Paul and his teaching style. He was an extremely knowledgeable person, and that quality influenced all the other aspects of his teaching style.

Paul Was Dialogical

Ill-informed teachers tend to fear the questions and comments of their students. One way to avoid them is to fill the time they are together with teacher-talk. Paul seemed to have no such fears and therefore had no need to do all the talking. On the other hand, it's quite apparent from Acts that Paul did his share. That's consistent with his overall approach. The teacher in the authority-enabler model is inclined to make verbal presentations. It's what happens *after* the presentation that determines whether a teacher using this model will be open to dialog.

The writer of Acts was concerned with telling the gospel through the words of St. Paul. He provides us with many of his presentations. We know considerably less about what his hearers said in response. Neither do we know how much of the conversation they were able to capture. There was no one standing in the wings with a Flanders Scale in hand, noting each time either the teacher or students spoke.

The flavor of Acts, however, suggests that Paul did his share of listening. The nature of his audience—many times adult Jewish males—supports that notion. And not to be overlooked is the repeated comment that Paul *argued* in defense of the gospel (Acts 17:2). Present understanding of the word *argue* is basically negative. It suggests verbal fights in which two or more people shout angrily at each other. There is nothing rational about it. Sometimes an argument begins as a conversation. One thing leads to another until temper and defensiveness degenerate the conversation into an "argument." Since this is all rather unpleasant, people tend to avoid arguments. That's true of teachers as well as students.

The writer of Acts didn't have the above understanding in mind when he wrote that Paul argued in defense of the gospel. What he meant to describe was a process in which one of the participants stated a proposition and then went on to defend it. Those who didn't accept the idea, or the supporting evidence, countered with their own. The exchange could go on over an extended period of time. Arguing required a thorough knowledge of one's own propositions and the willingness to hear and respond to those of others. The point of the argument was to defend one's position and, if possible, to persuade others of its truth. Basic to the process was a willingness not only to hear another view, but to take it seriously and deal with it in the context of one's own beliefs. Participants in the argument were expected to be logical, good listeners, knowledgeable, and persuasive. Respect for each other had to be taken for granted.

It's true that Paul's arguments sometimes turned into fights. On at least two occasions the fights turned into riots (Acts 14:5; 17:5ff.). These incidents demonstrate that there were times when the process broke down. One gets the impression, however, that this was due more to the frustrations of Paul's opponents than his failure to argue. Perhaps Paul's problem was that he argued only too well. Then, as now, there were people who didn't like to lose an argument. Then, as now, when words failed to convince, there were those who would turn to violence to prove a point. There were times when Paul appeared to have won the argument and then lost his opportunity to continue teaching in a particular place. Not content with forcing Paul to leave, some of these people followed him from town to town, serving as adversaries in new locations where Paul tried to preach and teach (Acts 15:1ff.; 17:10ff.). If Paul ever grew weary of the struggle, he had good reasons.

The basic point is that Paul's style took for granted interaction between himself and his hearers. For the most part he taught adult, informed people. He knew that they weren't going to change their thoughts and beliefs just because he said they should. He needed, further, to know what they were thinking, how they were responding to what he said and wrote. The only way he could know was to allow them to speak. This Paul did with the hope that those he taught would come to know the gospel. It was a part of his style.

Paul Cared for Those He Taught

According to one study, the most valued characteristic of a teacher is the ability to establish positive relationships with students. How teachers go about this is a matter of style. Some do it by being genuinely gentle and thoughtful. Others express interest in their students' activities. Still others gain respect because of the high expectations they have of themselves and their students. For most teachers it's a combination of traits that bring about this positive relationship. In a context of compulsory education one can well understand why this quality is so highly valued by both teachers and students.

Positive is not the best way to describe Paul's relationship with those he taught, but then his situation was not one in which anyone was required to accept him as a teacher. He was capable of evoking strong reactions to himself and what he taught. Some developed profoundly close ties with him and did as much as they could for him. Others were thoroughly alienated. Thus, if one were to evaluate his relationships, the results would have to be mixed. But if we focus on his attitude *toward* those he taught, the picture is clear. He cared for them—he cared a great deal. It might even be argued that he cared too much, and that became a problem for him. I don't think Paul could have understood that. He cared whatever the cost. That was his style.

There are several ways in which this characteristic is illustrated in his teaching. The most important is related to the outcomes that Paul looked for from his teaching. The results he hoped and worked for were worth all he had to give. He described those outcomes when he wrote:

> For I want you to know how greatly I strive for you, and for those at Laodicea, and for all who have not seen my face, that their hearts may be encouraged as they are knit together in love, to have all the riches of assured understanding and the knowledge of God's mystery, of Christ, in whom are hid all the treasures of wisdom and knowledge. I say this in order that no one may delude you with beguiling speech. For though I am absent in body, yet I am with you in spirit, rejoicing to see your good order and the firmness of your faith in Christ.
>
> As therefore you received Christ Jesus the Lord, so live in him, rooted and built up in him and established in faith, just as you were *taught,* abounding in thanksgiving (Col. 2:1-7, emphasis added).

The importance of the above outcomes is reflected in the way that Paul taught. One of those ways, as noted earlier, was argumentation. Others were exhortation, direction, pleading, and challenge. As often as he could, Paul found time to be with those he taught. He reminded the Ephesian elders of the hours he had spent with them—sometimes in tears (Acts 20:31). For many of his congregations he took the time to write letters of encouragement and instruction. Sometimes they were written in a spirit of gentleness (1 Thess. 2:7), but not always. Indignation led him to write: "O foolish Galatians! Who has bewitched you. . . ?" (Gal. 3:1).

Another dimension of Paul's care for his students is illustrated in his acceptance of them where they were in their development—even when they were more immature than he would have hoped (1 Cor. 3:1ff.). He knew that there was not much point in pursuing a more profound theology when they were still struggling with the basics. On the other hand, Paul wasn't content to let his learners remain where they were in their understanding. He expressed his love and care for them by challenging them to grow. "What we pray for," he wrote to the Corinthians, "is your improvement" (2 Cor. 13:9).

Paul's warnings about false teachers is another indication of his care for his students. He knew these teachers would come and that he would not always be present to deal with them. The churches would have to be ready to deal with this challenge on their own. Paul prepared the churches for this eventuality. First, he constantly taught the gospel with all the energy he had. He reinforced his teaching by remaining in some congregations over an extended period of time, by clarifying his theology through letters, and by pointing out errors when they occurred (1 Cor. 5:1ff.; 16:8). Second, he rejoiced with and commended those congregations that had grasped the meaning of the gospel (Rom. 1:8ff.).

Third, Paul pointed out the avenues of attack that the false teachers would take and encouraged his people to be faithful to what he had taught them (2 Cor. 11:12ff.; Gal. 2:4). Fourth, he did one of the most difficult things a teacher can do. He told his people that they must assume responsibility for faithfully teaching the gospel. If they were to be mature, they would have to assume the teaching function that had been Paul's. Paul seemed to realize that for this to happen he would have to separate himself from those for whom he cared so much (Acts 20:17-37).

Behind all of this, of course, was Paul's realization that these congregations weren't his at all—they were God's. Fifth, therefore, Paul showed his care for these people by his constant prayers in their behalf. In his prayer life he demonstrated the conviction that though he may have planted, watered, or harvested, it was God who gave the increase (1 Cor. 3:6). Paul trusted God to keep and care for the church. It was his style.

Finally, Paul expressed his care for his students by continuing to be interested in their development. While it's true that Paul realized that his people must assume responsibility for the teaching of the gospel where they were, he did not forget about them. In their behalf Paul assumed a function that is often forgotten— that of supervision. Though it isn't always recognized as such, supervision is one of the most caring acts a teacher, especially a teacher of teachers, can do for another. It sometimes happens in Christian education that once teachers are recruited for the church school, they aren't given any supervision. No one asks them how they are doing or whether they need any help. Few come around to give them encouragement. Those teachers are just there. They could be doing fine or floundering, they could be faithful to the gospel or teaching flagrant contradictions to it, but nobody really knows. That doesn't happen where teachers are cared for.

Paul was concerned for his congregations all through his life. He knew they were to become the teachers of the church. Much depended upon what happened in them. Most important was the message that was taught within them. Therefore he watched over his congregations, waited for news about them, and wrote to them as he saw their needs. One example of this is in 1 Thessalonians where he wrote:

> Therefore when we could bear it no longer, we were willing to be left behind at Athens alone, and we sent Timothy, our brother and God's servant in the gospel of Christ, to establish you in your faith and to exhort you, that no one be moved by these afflictions. You yourselves know that this is to be our lot. For when we were

with you, we told you beforehand that we were to suffer affliction; just as it has come to pass, and as you know. For this reason, when I could bear it no longer, I sent that I might know your faith, for fear that somehow the tempter had tempted you and that our labor would be in vain (1 Thess. 3:1-5).

The report Paul received in this case was positive, but it wasn't always that way. That's the way it is in teaching. Teachers don't always communicate as well as they would like. Students don't always grasp what they have been taught. The only way to find out if the learning objectives have been achieved is to inquire, and Paul was more than willing to do that. He couldn't afford to run the risk of not knowing if others had learned what he had taught. He wanted to know where things stood. That was part of his style.

Thus Paul could acknowledge the problems people were having in Corinth—their quarrels, immorality, confusion about the Lord's Supper and the resurrection, and all the rest. Each of these problems could have been viewed as an indication of Paul's failure as a teacher, or of his congregation's failure to learn. Paul, the congregation—or both—could have gotten weary of the struggle involved in learning and just given it up. But Paul didn't, and he wouldn't let the Corinthians give up either. He cared too much, and he expressed his care by trying again and again to teach in a way that others could understand.

There's no question that maintaining interest in those one has taught takes time and effort. It's easier to let students pass into one's life for a while, then to let them go in exchange for others for whom one is responsible for several months, or a year. That wasn't Paul's style. From his life and letters it's clear that he meant it when he wrote: "I will most gladly spend and be spent for your souls" (2 Cor. 12:15).

There are many ways teachers can express their care for students. Because Paul wasn't always gentle or affirming, there were probably times when he was not perceived as a caring person. That's a risk teachers have to take. It's in the long run, in terms of the anticipated outcomes, that a teacher's real concern for students is found. Again, unfortunately, some would use that argument to justify an authoritarian model built around the notion that the "end justifies the means." Paul would have had nothing to do with that. He knew Jesus, not Machiavelli. He would have argued that the end *determines* the way, and the most excellent way is love.

> If I speak in the tongues of men and of angels, but have not love, I am a noisy gong or a clanging symbol. And if I have prophetic powers, and understand all mysteries and all knowledge, and if I have all faith, so as to remove mountains, but have not love, I am nothing (1 Cor. 13:1-2).

He went on to describe that love:

> Love is patient and kind; love is not jealous or boastful; it is not arrogant or rude. Love does not insist on its own way; it is not irritable or resentful; it does not rejoice at wrong, but rejoices in the right. Love bears all things, believes all things, hopes all things, endures all things (1 Cor. 13:4-7).

The realization of love as Paul described it to the Corinthians is beyond any human possibility. He knew that it was beyond him. Yet it was to this love that Paul aspired. He pressed on toward the upward call of God in Christ Jesus—to the love of Jesus. In his striving others must have seen a glimpse of the love of which he spoke. Though unfinished and marred, Paul's style was to love and care for those he taught.

Paul Was Purposeful

Intentionality is a word that is used increasingly these days to describe a teacher's activity. Emphasis upon it suggests that there have been times when intent has been missing from instruction. That was not true of Paul. Whatever he did or said, one could be sure that sooner or later Paul would move in the direction of his purpose—the telling of the gospel. Paul gave classic expression to this commitment when he wrote to the Corinthians: "For I decided to know nothing among you except Jesus Christ and him crucified" (1 Cor. 2:2). Intentionality was Paul's style, and it was demonstrated in at least two ways in his teaching: in his ability to recognize a teachable moment and in his way of building on his learners' present knowledge.

Being intentional, Paul knew where to go to take advantage of teachable moments. On the Sabbath day he went to the Jewish synagogue. When he wasn't accepted there, he went out to other places where people gathered. In such a place, outside the walls of Philippi, Paul found Lydia. After his instruction she became one of the first converts to Christianity in Europe (Acts 16:11-15).

Being in the right place was only part of Paul's intentionality. In addition, he was always ready to speak when given the opportunity. The rulers of the synagogue in Antioch of Pisidia, after the reading of the Scriptures, invited Paul to bring a word of exhortation to the Sabbath gathering. Without any hesitation Paul launched into a review of Israel's history that ended with his telling of the resurrection of Jesus (Acts 13:13ff.).

Sure of his purpose, Paul also recognized teachable moments when they just happened to come his way. A bell didn't have to ring, or a series of classes be organized, for Paul to be about his work. A mob scene in Jerusalem, an earthquake in Philippi, an imprisonment in Rome, or the curiosity of a Roman governor were all opportunities, in the perception of Paul, to teach. He seized them when they came with an enthusiastic and daring intentionality.

Paul's assurance of purpose and his thorough knowledge of his subject allowed him to be sensitive to his audience. He had no need to put his learners down by an expression of his more superior knowledge. His purpose wasn't to draw attention to himself or the complexities of the gospel. He could have done either or both, but he didn't.

Though it sometimes happened, it wasn't Paul's intent to alienate his audience. In an attempt to avoid it, he sensitively built on what his learners already accepted to be true. This is illustrated in his contacts with both Jews and Gentiles. With the former he usually began his teaching by rehearsing the history of Israel. Then he would remind them of God's promise of a Messiah. (One can almost see the heads of his hearers nod in agreement with what he said.) Finally Paul came to what he had been leading up to all the time—his purpose. He told them that Jesus, the crucified and risen one, was the promised one. Having introduced Jesus as the Messiah, Paul went back over scriptural passages pointing out the necessity for the Messiah to die and rise again (Acts 13:16ff.; 17:1ff.; 19:8). In most cases Paul was well-received.

It's not likely that many Gentiles knew much of either Israel's history or its God. With them, obviously, Paul had to take a different tack, and he did. His experience in Athens is the best example. When he was invited to speak on the Areopagus, he began with an observation that most could have made: the Athenians were very religious, at least in their own way. Not willing to leave any stone unturned in their religious devotion, they had built an altar to an unknown god. It was to this altar that Paul drew their attention when he said to the Athenian philosophers: "What therefore you worship as unknown, this I proclaim to you" (Acts 17:23).

Having gained their attention, Paul continued in terms the Greeks could well appreciate. He spoke of a creator God in terms that must have kindled thoughts of Aristotle and his statements about an unmoved mover. He then argued that such a God could not be contained in a statue or anything else made with hands. Platonic idealism and Aristotelian logic would have supported this notion. Finally Paul spoke of Jesus and the resurrection. As the writer of Acts notes, this was offensive to many of the Greeks. After Paul mentioned it, most moved away from him, but *some* *believed* (Acts 17:22-34). Would there have been those "some" if Paul had not started from the common ground that both understood?

Wherever Paul went, among both Jews and Gentiles, there were some who responded in faith, who were ready to listen. A part of that readiness came about as a result of Paul's style of teaching. Educators now realize that adults (and Paul taught adults) are not especially open to having their beliefs and values challenged. Having made them a part of their lives, there is a strong inclination for adults to protect their convictions against what is foreign. People who attack those convictions are often seen as dangerous. Paul seemed to be aware of this, or at least taught as though he were. Affirming what his hearers already knew, he went on to give this knowledge the greater meaning of the gospel. It was all a part of his style.

Paul Was Faithful to the Gospel

The essence of teaching for Paul was the communication of the gospel—a communication that created saving faith in the one who received it. As an apostle, this was what Paul had been called to do—to tell the story of Jesus. If he hadn't been told how to do it, and if there were times when he wondered where he should do it, he didn't doubt that he must do it. Teaching was one way of making that story known. As Paul taught, he had one primary responsibility, that of being trustworthy of the charge that had been given to him (1 Cor. 4:1-2).

Some have argued that since faithfulness is the primary responsibility of the Christian teacher, no other quality is all that important. Such logic has been used to justify lazy and inept teaching. Some teachers have convinced themselves that they can get along with the same old methods, materials, and jokes that they have used for years—just so they remain faithful to the message. Others seem to think that it's all right for teachers to drone on and on without enthusiasm or interest—just as long as they are faithful. That's not at all what Paul meant. One gets a better understanding of his meaning when the passage from Corinthians is enlarged with the following from Colossians:

> Him [Jesus] we proclaim, warning every man and teaching every man in all wisdom, that we may present every man mature in Christ. For this I toil, striving with all the energy which he mightily inspires within me (Col. 1:28-29).

Clearly, for Paul, faithfulness to the gospel was not an invitation to relax but a motivation to serve with all the gifts that God had given.

Nevertheless, Paul did submit himself in faith under the authority of the gospel. This, above all, characterized his teaching. Wherever he went, whomever he met, under whatever circumstances he lived, whichever approach he would take in his teaching—whom he served and what he taught remained the same. Having been given a trust, his style would reflect every effort to be found worthy.

For Reflection

1. What teaching style has been most helpful to you in your own education? Think of particular teachers who have been able to assist and encourage you to learn. Describe them.
2. If you are a teacher, how do you think your students would describe your teaching style? Is this the perception you want them to have of you?
3. Compare/contrast your responses to 1 and 2 above with the description of Paul's teaching style given in this chapter.
4. Do you think Paul's teaching style is a valid one for teachers to adopt today? What reasons can you give for your responses?

CHAPTER SEVEN

A CLOSING COMMENT

Teachers are public persons. They have chosen to involve themselves in the lives and thoughts of those they teach. As they do, they are given identity and definition in the minds of their students. They take on a personality and an image that may or may not be consistent with reality or the teacher's own self-image.

Paul seemed to have been aware of this and did all he could to present a clear and consistent pattern of himself for his students to see. Whether it was to the Galatians, the Corinthians, or any other congregation, Paul concealed neither his thoughts nor his feelings. As he taught the gospel he also shared with his people his hopes, his motivation, his fears, his dreams, and his love. He wanted those he taught to know him as well as the content he would have them learn.

Whether he did this self-consciously, as one would apply a theory or a model learned in an education class, is beside the point. Paul did it intuitively. He did it because he was a person who could only function out of his wholeness. In this study I have attempted to describe, in a more or less analytical way, aspects of Paul's teaching: his purpose, his view of the learner and learning, his style, and his sense of accountability in his teaching ministry. Having done so, however, I would hope that he would be seen in his wholeness—as one who had learned to live by the grace of God and who had no other purpose than to help others do the same. I think that's the way, finally, Paul would want to be perceived as a teacher.

In writing this book it has been my intent that those teachers in the church today who read it will have been given an occasion to reflect on their own teaching as well as that of Paul's. It is hoped the outcome of that reflection will be greater wholeness in what they are about in their teaching ministry.

Put on then, as God's chosen ones, holy and beloved, compassion, kindness, lowliness, meekness, and patience, forbearing one another and, if one has a complaint against another, forgiving each other; as the Lord has forgiven you, so you also must forgive. And above all these put on love, which binds everything together in perfect harmony. And let the peace of Christ rule in your hearts, to which indeed you were called in the one body. And be thankful. Let the word of Christ dwell in you richly, teach and admonish one another in all wisdom, and sing psalms and hymns and spiritual songs with thankfulness in your hearts to God. And whatever you do, in word or deed, do everything in the name of the Lord Jesus, giving thanks to God the Father through him (Col. 3:12-17).